Jaime Sucher

Shih Tzu

Everything about Purchase,
Care, Nutrition, and Behavior

Full-color Photographs
Illustrations by
Michele Earle-Bridges

BARRON'S

2 CONTENTS

SHOULD YOU BUY A SHIH TZU?

An Intelligent Choice

Since you are reading this book, it would be safe to assume that you either have a dog or are considering getting one. This is by no means an unusual act. Long ago, our ancestors learned how to domesticate this wonderful creature, and as a result, the companion dog has become part of our culture. For nearly 14,000 years, man and dog have been living together. At first, the dog was valued as a hunter; as time went on, their immense loyalty made them valued protectors of human life, property, flocks, and herds. While in modern times we still make use of them as hunters, herders, and protectors, our relationship with dogs has gone well beyond that of owner and worker. Dogs have become our dearest companions and our favorite pets.

The toy-dog group can be considered the furthest extension of our emotional ties to dogs. Unlike other breeds that were originally bred to tend sheep, retrieve fallen prey, or rescue injured people, the toy dogs were developed strictly for the purpose of pleasure. While some of them do make excellent watchdogs, the members of this group were simply designed to be house pets and companions.

The Shih Tzu's compact size makes it the perfect house pet.

One of the oldest of the toy breeds is the Shih Tzu (pronounced Sheed-zoo). The origins of this breed can be traced back to China where it appears in artwork and texts dating back to early in the seventh century. The name, Shih Tzu, means "Lion Dog" in Chinese; however, this is a very deceptive name indeed. This dog was not bred to hunt lions, nor does the name refer in any way to its personality. Instead, the dog was given this name because it resembled the lion as depicted in traditional oriental art.

As a companion dog, the Shih Tzu has some excellent credentials. It was the favorite house pet of the royal family during the Manchu Dynasty. Also, shortly after its introduction into England, it became the dog of choice among many lords and ladies, including the Countess of Essex.

The same virtues that have made this breed the choice of royalty have likewise been the reason for the Shih Tzu's recent increase in popularity. The diminutive size that characterizes the breed makes it the ideal choice for urban life. It makes an excellent apartment dog, especially for someone who is living alone or without children. This is a breed that cannot live alone in kennels, but flourishes in the society of human beings.

The Shih Tzu is a small, compact breed. It is also very hardy and sound. It is a long-haired breed, whose coat comes in a wide variety of colors and patterns. Underneath all its hair, the Shih Tzu hides large, drooping ears, short legs, a broad, sturdy body, and a short muzzle.

The Shih Tzu is a lively and vivacious dog, intelligent, very alert, and of general good temper. Like most of the toy breeds, the Shih Tzu is proud, and at times seems even haughty or arrogant. Shih Tzu have a keen sense of themselves and at times are extremely self-centered. The overall personality of the Shih Tzu to many may, in fact, seem "undoglike," and more on the lines of a spoiled child. The owner of the Shih Tzu, however, likes to refer to the dog's personality as "totally human," and attributes to this the reason for the breed's success.

If you are considering the purchase of a Shih Tzu, you should think your decision over very carefully; owning any dog is a responsibility that should not be taken lightly. There are all too many people who have rashly purchased a dog without being aware of, or prepared for, the needs of the animal. The result of these impulsive acts is usually an unhappy owner and an equally sad dog. So before you consider buying a Shih Tzu, review the following information carefully, and answer the questions openly and honestly. The answers will dictate whether or not you are ready to own a Shih Tzu.

Do you have, or are you planning to have, any small children in your home? If the answer is yes, then you are well advised to avoid getting a Shih Tzu (as well as most other toy dogs). Many of the traits that make the Shih Tzu such a popular dog make it a poor choice as the pet of a new and growing family. The Shih Tzu may become jealous of a small child and vie for attention. In addition, the small size of the breed does not allow it to stand up physically to the rough and tumble abuse that it will inevitably receive from a rambunctious child.

Are you the nervous type or easily excitable? The Shih Tzu is a very active and alert dog, becoming at times nervous or excited. During these times, they may run around and bark a lot. While one may consider these good watchdog qualities, they can easily be upsetting to some people.

Do you have the time, patience, and energy needed to properly raise a dog? The long-haired Shih Tzu requires daily grooming, and puppies need to be trained and housebroken.

Are you willing to devote some of your free time to the dog? Shih Tzu need human companionship for their emotional well-being. If you travel a lot, or take long vacations away from home, you must be willing either to take the dog with you, or find a sitter for your pet.

Do you intend to keep your dog in an outdoor kennel? The Shih Tzu is a house dog, and therefore must be kept indoors. While it is good to take your Shih Tzu outdoors for exercise, you must not expose it to harsh weather for a prolonged period of time. Shih Tzu are not very tolerant of cold weather.

Do you understand the long-term commitment of owning a Shih Tzu? A dog may live with you for almost as long as a child, and will most likely spend more time at home. The life span of this breed is ordinarily 12 years, and is sometimes much longer.

Finally, can you afford to keep a Shih Tzu? In addition to the initial purchase of the dog, you will need to buy supplies. Food alone can cost as much as $30 per month. You will also have to pay for those annual visits to the veterinarian.

As the owner of a dog, you are responsible

for it in every way. A dog's health and soundness are dependent upon its owner feeding it properly and giving it all the medical care it needs. Also, the way your dog behaves depends on how well you train it. As you can see, there is much to consider before you buy a Shih Tzu.

If you need answers to any other questions, or if you wish to talk to a local breeder before making your decision, then contact the Shih Tzu Club of America (STCA). (For address see Information, page 92.) They can supply you with a list of registered breeders and the address of the nearest chapter of the STCA.

Adult or Puppy?

There is little question as to why four out of every five people desiring to purchase a dog begin by looking for a puppy rather than an adult dog. Just one look at a litter of Shih Tzu puppies will tell you why. How can anyone resist wanting one after they see those tiny, clumsy balls of fur frolicking with their littermates in such a carefree manner? A single glimpse can melt the coldest heart.

Indeed, one of the greatest pleasures of owning a Shih Tzu puppy is to watch it grow from this small, delicate bundle of energy into a proud, dignified, and intelligent member of the family. This, however, takes a lot of patience, time, and energy. Puppies need constant care. They must be fed more frequently and watched more carefully than adult dogs, and need to be trained and housebroken.

For those who cannot give a puppy all that it needs, choosing an adult would be much more advantageous. By getting an adult dog, you can free yourself from the drudgeries of housebreaking chores and rigorous feeding schedules. The adult Shih Tzu would also be a benefit to anyone who does not have enough flexibility in their daily schedule to accommodate a helpless puppy.

An adult Shih Tzu will usually adapt easily to a new owner and environment, and would make an ideal pet for the elderly, or anyone else for whom raising a puppy would be too much work. The greatest drawback to buying an adult Shih Tzu is that it may be difficult to correct any bad habits that it may have previously acquired.

The choice, then, is evenly divided between obtaining an older dog that would doubtless be easier to care for, or getting a puppy and raising it to adapt to one's own lifestyle and more easily gain its loyalty and devotion. If you are looking to obtain a show dog, however, the choice may become one of monetary feasibility.

There is a certain amount of luck involved in buying a potential show puppy. While you can check the puppy's lineage, and you can see the conformation of the dam (mother), you cannot be sure that the puppy will grow up with the desired looks and temperament. In fact, the Shih Tzu does not reach full maturity or beauty until the age of almost three years. On the other hand, if you wish to purchase a proven adult show dog, it will cost a significantly greater amount of money.

Male or Female?

Another choice you will have to make when choosing your Shih Tzu is whether to get a male or a female. This is usually an easier choice, for it is more a matter of personal preference. In Shih Tzu, there are only slight differences in the temperaments of males and females. Females are usually more even-tempered except when

they are in season, while males may become more irritable from time to time. There is little difference when it comes to training, although females do tend to be slightly friendlier, while males will be more ruggedly independent. These differences are so slight that unless you have raised both sexes simultaneously you might not even notice them.

Where the choice of male or female becomes more important, however, is if you decide that you want to raise puppies. If you are considering starting a kennel, then you would want a female. If you plan to buy a second Shih Tzu and you already have a male, sometimes bringing a second male home may lead to fights (although bringing home a female may lead to other obvious problems). If you have a female you can get another female without worries.

If you are interested in raising puppies, you should choose a female Shih Tzu.

If you select a female and have no intention of breeding her, then have her spayed. There is an alarming number of unwanted and homeless dogs in the United States, and every precaution a dog owner can take to prevent unwanted pregnancies should be taken. The spayed female is also less likely to suffer from breast tumors, ovarian cysts, false pregnancies, and other ailments. Likewise, male dogs should be neutered. Neutered males are less likely to develop testicular or prostate cancer.

If you plan on entering a conformation dog show, do not have your dog spayed or neutered because it will be immediately disqualified.

When you bring your puppy home, try to avoid causing it undue stress.

Buying a Shih Tzu

The first step in buying a Shih Tzu is to obtain a list of the reputable breeders in your area. You can get this list by writing to the Shih Tzu Club of America or the American Kennel Club (AKC) (see page 92). Make appointments to visit as many of these breeders as possible. Alternatively, you may visit your local pet dealer. Well-run pet shops generally obtain their puppies from good breeders. While pet dealers do not carry all breeds of dogs at all times, they are in contact with breeders, and are sometimes able to supply quality Shih Tzu puppies on demand.

Your first concern should be the health of the puppy you choose.

When visiting each store or breeder, you should inspect their dogs and the conditions in which they are kept. While it will be difficult to walk away from the first cuddly, furry puppies you see, it is advisable to visit as many stores and/or breeders as possible, regardless of the distance. It is extremely important to obtain a healthy and well-cared-for puppy. A sickly, poorly raised puppy may need extensive medical care, and may not properly develop physically and/or emotionally. By finding the right dog at the beginning, you can save yourself a great deal of effort, money, and heartbreak later on.

During your inspection, make sure that the premises in which the puppies are kept are clean and that the puppies have an ample amount of room to move about. Watch the puppies interact with each other to see if they seem happy and healthy. Observe the coat condition and overall appearance of the puppies and the mother. These are all indicators of the quality of the operation.

In the world of dogs, one finds that the highest-quality pets are offered by the best and most conscientious dealers and breeders. They are, therefore, usually more expensive. Never be tempted to buy a "cheap" dog. Shih Tzu that are offered at bargain prices are usually no bargain at all. It is more than likely that there is something wrong with them. These dogs may be in poor health, or may have been raised strictly for profit by an inexperienced or unscrupulous breeder.

So take your time. Talk to all the breeders and pet dealers in detail. Be thorough in your investigation of their premises and breeding stock. Most breeders will even give you the names of others who have bought Shih Tzu from them. Call these references to see if they are satisfied. Then, once you are confident in your choice of breeder, it is time to select a puppy that will suit your purposes and fit in with your lifestyle.

Selecting a Puppy

Choosing a Shih Tzu puppy that is to become a house pet and member of your family is much different from selecting a potential show dog. In either case, emphasis should be placed on the overall health of the puppy.

A healthy puppy will have a clean, smooth, and shiny coat. Its ears should be clean of any type of discharge. The puppy's eyes should be clear and bright. Feel the puppy's body and legs. You should feel the solidity of the body muscles and the strong leg bones. Lift the puppy's hair and examine its skin. It should be moist and smooth, and free from flakes or scales. You should also examine the condition of the puppy's mother.

Once you feel confident about the health of the puppies and the quality of the breeder, it is time to choose the right puppy for you. If you are looking strictly for a family pet, then it becomes a matter of personal choice, and in many cases the puppy may pick you.

If you are looking for a potential show puppy, then you should be concerned with more than just the puppy's health. One of the keys to selecting a potential show dog is examining the puppy's pedigree papers. These papers are a written record of the dog's more recent ancestry, and indicate all show champions in its lineage. Although there is no guarantee that a puppy who is a descendent of championship stock will also be a winner, the odds will at least be better than if you obtained a puppy that has no proven ancestry.

If the puppy's pedigree and health are satisfactory, then you should look for a puppy with the proper show temperament. Shih Tzu that are exhibited in dog shows should be active, alert, and carry themselves with the distinctive arrogance that characterizes the breed.

Once you have selected your Shih Tzu, ask the breeder for the date the puppy was wormed, and be sure to get a written record for your veterinarian of this and any vaccinations it may have received. Never be afraid to ask breeders questions. A good breeder is just as concerned as you are about making sure his or her puppies get the best treatment. Always keep a line of communication open.

When you finally complete the purchase of your new Shih Tzu puppy you should receive its AKC registration certificate (or an application form to fill out), its pedigree papers, and a health certificate from the breeder's veterinarian. If the puppy has already received its formal registered show name from its breeder, then you should complete the transfer by sending the registration certificate (AKC papers) and the appropriate fee to the American Kennel Club. After they complete the transfer of ownership to you, they will send you a new certificate. If the puppy has not been named, then you will complete the application, choose the dog's formal name, and send it with the fee to the AKC.

Bringing Your Puppy Home

As a general rule, the earlier you can bring your new puppy home, the easier it will be for it to adapt to its new environment. Also, the younger the puppy, the less likely the chances of it picking up any bad habits that the new owner may find hard to break. On the other hand, the puppy must be old enough to eat and drink on its own.

The optimum age at which a Shih Tzu puppy should be brought into its new home is seven weeks. A seven-week-old puppy should have little trouble adapting to its new environment. Recent studies have indicated that puppies are very sensitive to changes in their surroundings during their eighth week. By placing a puppy in its new home at seven weeks, you can avoid any undue stress or behavioral problems that may occur. These studies also suggest that if you cannot bring the puppy home earlier, then it would be best to wait until the ninth week.

Expenses

The purchase price of a top-quality Shih Tzu will vary; however, you should expect to pay at least $250. Naturally, puppies from champion-caliber parents may sell for $1,000 or more. In general, the younger the dog, the less expensive it is because the breeder has invested less time and money in it.

As stated earlier, food may cost as much as $30 a month. You will also need to purchase special equipment for feeding, housing, and grooming your new dog. Your Shih Tzu will require annual immunizations against all infectious diseases. Additional veterinary costs may occur if your dog gets sick or injured.

In many townships there are fees that must be paid in order to obtain a license for your dog. There are also the fees you will have to pay to register your dog with the American Kennel Club, as well as the annual dues should you decide to join the Shih Tzu Club of America.

As you can see, the costs of owning a Shih Tzu go far beyond the initial purchase price. Consider this carefully before deciding to buy.

HOUSING AND SUPPLIES

Indoor Requirements

As previously mentioned, the Shih Tzu is considered a house dog. Therefore, the majority of its life will be spent indoors. The small size of this breed allows the Shih Tzu to adapt to life in a city apartment just as easily as it would in a big country home.

Keep in mind, however, that dogs are territorial animals and their behavior and mental well-being are greatly affected by their environment. Making sure that your Shih Tzu has the proper indoor space requirements is the first step in assuring the proper adjustment of your pet to its new environment. Dogs that are subject to cramped living quarters, or are not given an area where they can sleep undisturbed, can become stressed and nervous. This in turn can lead to changes in biological functions, including digestive and excretory problems.

While most indoor dogs are allowed to have the run of the house, it is important that your Shih Tzu be given two special areas in your home in which it will remain relatively undisturbed. These are its eating and sleeping areas.

Your Shih Tzu's eating area should be located in an easy-to-clean part of your home. Rooms that have tile or linoleum floors, such as a kitchen or bathroom, are usually the best. Once this location is chosen it should not be changed.

In addition to food and water bowls, leashes and collars, your dog will need the proper toys for playtime.

If you do not have any rooms in your home with an easy-to-clean floor, you can buy a small piece of linoleum and place it under your dog's food dishes. The location of the food and water dishes should allow your Shih Tzu to eat in peace. If you put the dishes near a wall or in a corner, away from frequently traveled paths, it will give the dog the peace it needs to eat and digest its meals properly.

The sleeping area, like the feeding area, should be placed to allow your Shih Tzu to sleep or rest without being disturbed. The best sleeping areas are in the corners of rooms that are not subject to heavy human traffic. Corners are good because they offer your dog protection on two sides, creating a more comfortable and secure feeling. The corner you choose should be draft-free and have direct sunlight.

Try to select an area that will make it easy for you to confine your dog's movements. When you are away from home, or when you go to sleep, you may wish to prevent your Shih Tzu from having access to the entire house. In these cases, your dog will need to be confined to a part of your home that will give it free access to its eating and sleeping areas.

The temperature of your Shih Tzu's sleeping area is also important. An adult Shih Tzu needs the sleeping area to be kept about 70°F (21°C), while a puppy requires a warmer climate of about 75°F (24°C). Puppies are more susceptible to catching colds, so the sleeping area should be located away from heat sources, and not subject to excessive increases or decreases in temperature.

Your Shih Tzu's sleeping area should be equipped with either a sleeping box and pad or a cage with a pad. Although you should make this choice in advance, I recommend using a cage because of its many benefits.

Before domestication, dogs were cave-dwelling animals. Instinctively, the modern dog finds security in any cave-like structure, once familiar with it. If you choose a cage, you will find that your dog will actually prefer to sleep there and will return on its own. The cage can also be used as a housebreaking aid (see the chapter entitled Basic and Advanced Training, page 90), traveling crate, and can also prove useful, for short periods, when you are unable to supervise your puppy. The cage can also serve as an invaluable training tool. If your puppy refuses to listen to your commands, you can pick it up and put it in its cage. After being involuntarily separated from its family, your Shih Tzu will quickly learn that you are unhappy with its performance.

The cage should be approximately 18 inches (46 cm) high, by 18 inches wide, by 24 inches (61 cm) long. The cage welds should be strong enough to resist the efforts of an active puppy. Should you choose to use a cage, it will also act as the puppy's house when you are not around to supervise it. This cage should be large enough to house your Shih Tzu, and yet be easy to handle when you travel or need to take your dog to the veterinarian.

If you decide not to use a cage, then you will need a sleeping box. The box should be large enough to accommodate a full-grown, stretched-out dog. Place a plastic liner and some cedar shavings on the bottom of the box (just in case of accidents) and an old blanket or pad on top.

If you decide to purchase a sleeping box, avoid those made of wicker or soft wood. An active Shih Tzu puppy, despite its small size, is capable of chewing them apart. Likewise, avoid boxes that are painted or stained. Many of these coatings are toxic, so unless you are absolutely positive about the harmlessness of the materials used, it is better to be safe than sorry. If you decide to build your own sleeping box, then the same rules apply. Use only nonsplintering hard-woods, and avoid using any paints or stains.

It is extremely important to keep your dog's sleeping area clean, especially if you have a puppy. Puppies have a low resistance to disease because their immune system is not fully developed. Everything you put into your puppy's sleeping box should be clean.

The Great Outdoors

Shih Tzu are house pets and should never be left outdoors for a long time. As a matter of fact, the only time your Shih Tzu needs to be outside is during exercise periods or when it has to do its "business." Even at these times, your dog should be closely supervised.

Unless you have a fenced-in yard that is Shih Tzu-proof, your dog should be on a leash when it is outdoors. If you do have a fenced-in yard, and you wish to allow your dog to run free, you should still take your Shih Tzu for walks and allow it to relieve itself away from your prop-erty. If not, your dog may feel that it can relieve itself any place it chooses, and before long your entire yard can become quite messy and full of unpleasant odors. Your Shih Tzu will also appre-ciate its yard being kept clean. It is equally important that your Shih Tzu learns to behave just as well outdoors as it does indoors.

Under no circumstances should you consider keeping your Shih Tzu in an outdoor doghouse or a confining run. Generations upon generations of Shih Tzu have been bred to be companion animals. Much of their character and personality has been shaped by their heritage as house pets. If your Shih Tzu is to develop into the mature, self-confident dog that it is intended to be, it will need to be raised indoors, like any other member of your family.

During the cold winter months, the outdoor activity of your dog should be limited to your routine walks. While the Shih Tzu is a long-haired breed, it does not withstand the cold very well. Its undercoat lacks some of the insulating quality of other dogs, especially those of the hunting or working breeds. This is a result of their being bred as indoor pets for so long.

Finally, when you take your dog for its leashed walks, remember that you are completely responsible for your dog's actions. Do not allow your pet to wander around the neighbor's garden while you turn your head the other way. After all, nobody wants to wake up and find an unexpected and unwanted present on their lawn. Take your dog to an uninhabited area and allow it to relieve itself. You should also be aware that in many areas it is required by law that you clean up after your dog. Even if you live in an area where it is legal, you should prevent your dog from relieving itself in open and public areas.

Additional Accessories

Bringing home a new Shih Tzu puppy or adult will surely be an exciting and hectic event in any household. In order to prevent any excessive confusion from occurring on the big day, there are a few supplies you should purchase beforehand. Being prepared ahead of time will help you avoid having to make any trips away from home. It is very important that your puppy not be left alone during those first few days when it is adjusting to its new environment.

Among the most important equipment you will need are your dog's food and water dishes. These items come in a variety of sizes and can be made of different materials, which include metal, ceramic, glass, and plastic. When choosing these dishes, keep in mind that a Shih Tzu is a small breed whose head, when standing, is barely inches above the ground. Pick dishes that are not more than 3 inches (7.5 cm) deep. If you are feeding a puppy, you will have to use a very shallow bowl, or even a plate. The idea is to select feeding dishes that will allow your pet free access to its food and water. In addition, the dishes that you choose should be made in such a shape as to prevent tipping. Despite their diminutive size, a Shih Tzu with a voracious appetite may attempt to "wolf down" your culinary concoctions. If the bowls are not tip-proof, it could result in a real mess.

The choice of material from which the dishes are made is really a matter of personal preference. The only warnings to be given concern ceramic bowls. If you buy a ceramic bowl, be sure it is designed for food use. Some ceramic pieces are fired using a lead-based glaze. Bowls that are coated in these materials can result in lead poisoning if they are used over a long period of time. If you plan to clean your dog's bowls in a dishwasher, make sure they are made of a material that is dishwasher safe.

Two pieces of equipment that you will need when you first go and pick up your Shih Tzu

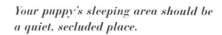

*Your puppy's sleeping area should be
a quiet, secluded place.*

one collar. Both nylon and leather collars will deteriorate with age, so you should check them from time to time. If you choose to use a metal collar, be sure it is not too heavy or too bulky. In addition, this type should only be used on an adult Shih Tzu, and not a puppy—puppies are not capable of handling the extra weight of a chain collar. Another type of collar that you might want to purchase is a choke-style collar. These can come in handy when the time arrives to train your puppy and teach it the basic commands.

Leashes, like collars, are also made of nylon, leather, or chain. Because you need have little fear of your Shih Tzu's body strength, there is really no need for a chain leash at any time. You can find an adequately strong leather leash in just about all sizes. If you are considering using a metal leash anyway, keep in mind that a Shih Tzu puppy will, more likely than not, chew on anything it can get within its tiny but ever so active jaws. If this should happen, chewing on a metal chain can damage the puppy's teeth.

There are several types of leashes available, and the styles you choose are dependent upon your intended uses. For regular walks, you need a leash that is only a few feet long. Never use an extremely long leash when you are out for a stroll. A short leash will enable you to bring the dog to your side quickly should the need

are a collar and a leash. The Shih Tzu, whether a puppy or an adult, does not require a strong collar made of chain. In fact, they need a lightweight collar, preferably made of nylon or leather. If you look carefully, you should be able to find one that is adjustable enough to fit both a puppy and a full-grown Shih Tzu. During the life of your dog, however, you may have to purchase more than

*Make sure the toys that you give your
Shih Tzu are suitable for small dogs.*

*This Shih Tzu is relaxing outside after an
exercise period.*

arise. If you give the dog any extra leeway
when you are out for a walk, you are only ask-
ing for trouble. There is always the chance of
your dog bolting into a busy street, and if you
are using an extra-long leash, you may be helpless to prevent a tragedy. If you wish to restrict
the movements of your Shih Tzu to a certain
part of your yard, a 30-foot (10-m) leash
with an automatic reel may prove useful.

There are other ways of restricting your
dog's outdoor range as well. One method

*Your Shih Tzu should always have a toy
to chew on.*

is to attach your dog's leash to a pulley that is set up to slide back and forth on a strong line strung between two trees. You can also create other ways yourself, but be sure that they do not jeopardize your dog's safety. Under no circumstances should you leave your Shih Tzu unsupervised for any lengthy period of time while attached to a collar and leash.

There are other supplies that you may wish to purchase for safety reasons. Reflecting tags and tape, which attach to your dog's leash and collar, can be of great help in making both the dog and owner more visible to car drivers at night. This makes nighttime walks much safer. It is also advisable to attach an identity tag to your dog's collar. This inexpensive item, which should contain your name, address, and telephone number, can prove to be invaluable should your dog ever be lost.

Another item you should have for safety reasons is a muzzle. In all my years as a dog owner, I am thankful that I have never had to use a muzzle, but I still keep one in a handy spot, just in case. Muzzles can be very helpful in handling an injured dog. Any dog, regardless of its size, may act unpredictably when it is in severe pain. If you must take a dog that is seriously hurt to the veterinarian, a muzzle can be a good precaution. When buying a muzzle, make sure that it can be adjusted for size to fit both an adult and a puppy. If you are planning to take your dog abroad, you may have to get a muzzle because some foreign countries require that all dogs wear them.

As a dog owner, it is almost inevitable that you will eventually have to deal with the problem of fleas or other external parasites. You should therefore keep some flea control products, a pair of tweezers, and some rubbing alcohol on hand. The recent scientific advances in flea-control medications and pesticide products for household use are extremely numerous and described in more detail later in this book. You will need the tweezers to remove ticks properly, and rubbing alcohol to disinfect the wound.

The flea-control method you choose will depend on several variables including the climate and the severity of the infestation. However, you will probably need to control these pests both on your Shih Tzu and in the areas of your house and yard that your dog frequents. The advice of a veterinarian or a professional dog groomer can be very helpful when trying to choose the right method(s) of treatment.

Dog Toys

While most dogs are supplied with adequate toys, most owners fail to understand their importance in maintaining both the physical and psychological well-being of their pets. Dogs, especially puppies, like children, need toys. Toys prevent your dog's life from becoming too tedious. Toys mean playtime! They let your puppy know that there is more to life than eating, sleeping, and training. Giving your Shih Tzu a toy will allow it to work out and burn up extra energy, thus giving the dog some of the exercise it needs. Toys also allow your dog to relieve any frustrations that may have been building.

Dog toys will also help your puppy sharpen its survival instincts. Some dogs treat their toys as if they were potential prey. They will attempt to track them down. They will try to sneak around behind their prey and crouch, waiting until the moment is right. Finally the puppy will attack. If all goes right, your puppy will render the toy harmless, and carry it around, victorious. Once this is done, your Shih Tzu may repeat the act all over again. Even hundreds of years of domestication are not enough to rid your dog of this instinctive behavior.

Should you still doubt the importance of dog toys, there is one other good reason to use them. Shih Tzu puppies are energetic and industrious little bundles of mischief. One way or the other, your puppy will find something to play with. If it is not a chew toy, then it might be the slender leg of your new coffee table. If it is not a tennis ball, then it might be your fuzzy slippers. If it is not a squeaky toy, then it might be your checkbook.

From the time a puppy begins to teethe until it reaches a ripe old age, it should always have a chewable toy to gnaw on. The best types of chew toys are rawhide bones. As your puppy gnaws, the rawhide becomes soft enough to prevent damage to the teeth. At the same time, this helps to strengthen your Shih Tzu's jaw muscles. Make sure you get a bone small enough for your puppy to handle properly, and be sure to replace it before the bone becomes small enough for the puppy to swallow whole. Never give your dog any toy that can break, crack, splinter, or shred. The resulting smaller pieces may be swallowed and cause choking or a blockage of the digestive tract.

All of your Shih Tzu's toys should be suitable for such a small breed of dog. Also, be sure that they are made from materials that are completely nontoxic. Never give your dog anything made from soft woods, or any painted items. Some older types of paint contain lead

that may be harmful if swallowed. Varnished or stained toys may also be potentially toxic and therefore should be avoided.

Incidentally, not all dog toys have to be store bought. Tennis balls, although too large for your Shih Tzu to get in its mouth, can still be pushed and rolled around. An empty cardboard box or shopping bag can be the source of much fun and adventure for a curious puppy. Feel free to be creative, only remember to use your common sense as well. Do not allow your Shih Tzu to play with anything small enough to swallow, or made from any material that it can pulverize.

As a final thought on dog toys, I will resort to a story as told to me by a friend. It seems that my friend had just purchased a new puppy (although not a Shih Tzu), and had been acclimating it to life in its new environment. One day, in his attempts to keep his new little friend entertained, he got an old slipper from his closet and began a game of tug-of-war. As it turned out, the dog became very fond of that slipper and of playing their new game. Unfortunately, the puppy's newfound fondness for footwear did not stop there. One day upon returning home from a long day's work, my friend found himself in need of an entire new wardrobe of footwear. Almost every shoe, sneaker, or slipper that carried his scent had been thoroughly chewed or slobbered upon. Luckily, the dog survived. The moral of this story is to be selective about the items you give to your puppy to use as toys. To a Shih Tzu puppy, there is little difference between your old slippers and your new ones. This goes for any object that may carry your scent.

Preparations

In addition to purchasing your equipment and supplies in advance, there are other ways of preparing yourself and your home in order to make your puppy's transition easier. Aside from the food and water dishes, collar, leash, toys, and bedding supplies, you will also need the proper grooming supplies. (These will be explained later in this chapter.) In addition, you will also want to pick up an adequate supply of puppy food. Use the same food that your puppy's breeder used. Changing the puppy's food during this emotional time increases the chances of dietary upsets.

Once this is done, it is time to puppy-proof your home. Puppy-proofing is the act of taking all potential hazards in your home and putting them out of the puppy's reach. Remove all poisons, including paints, cleaners, pesticides, and disinfectants. Store these in an area that is inaccessible to the puppy. Another poison that should be kept out of reach is antifreeze. There is evidently something about the smell of antifreeze that attracts dogs and cats. Unfortunately, it can be very harmful to your pet.

You must also remove all sharp objects such as nails, staples, and broken glass. If you own an older home, make sure you remove all flaking paint or paint chips. Older paints contain lead that, if ingested, can be harmful to both humans and animals.

Puppies are very curious creatures and they will explore any place that they have access to.

Finally, all electrical wires should be moved out of your puppy's reach. A dog that chews on electrical wires can be injured or killed by the resulting shock. If you are in doubt as to whether or not an object is within your dog's reach, it would be best to move the object and not take any chances. Remember that puppies are very curious creatures. They will roam through a house and explore every last inch that they can possibly get to. A puppy will sniff, paw, and attempt to chew on almost everything it encounters. In addition, do not take the small size of your Shih Tzu puppy for granted. It will use its lack of stature to its advantage by getting into every nook and cranny it can find.

Adjustment

It is inevitable that your puppy will experience a certain amount of loneliness during its first few days in your home. Prior to moving, the puppy felt safe and secure with its brothers and sisters, knowing that its mother's watchful eyes were always upon it. Now it is alone in a strange world that is full of unusual sights and sounds. This type of stress would affect anyone, let alone a tiny, defenseless, and very impressionable seven-week-old puppy.

Make your puppy's first day in its new home a quiet one. Let it know it is entering a calm, safe, and secure environment. Speak to your new friend in a soft, reassuring tone. Let it know that there is nothing to fear, that it will be taken care of. The last thing your puppy

CHECKLIST

Rules of Puppy Safety

Before bringing your new puppy home, review the following rules with your family and friends. In addition to preventing injury, these rules will help your puppy feel comfortable and safe in its new home and help increase its confidence in you and your family.

1 Avoid unnecessary excitement. Let the puppy adjust to its new surroundings.

2 Prohibit rough play. Puppies are very fragile creatures and should be handled with care.

3 Avoid picking up the puppy too much. Let it do its own walking as much as possible. This will allow it to get its exercise and to improve its motor skills.

4 Be sure everyone in your household knows the proper way to lift and carry your puppy. The proper technique is described in detail later in this chapter.

5 Do not subject your puppy to unnecessary heights because of the risk of falling. When it is necessary to place the puppy on an elevated surface, such as when you are examining or grooming it, someone must be present the entire time to ensure the puppy's safety.

6 Do not give bones or other hard objects to a young puppy. Until a puppy reaches about six months of age, it has only its milk teeth and cannot chew hard objects.

7 Try not to leave the puppy unsupervised during the first few weeks.

needs is to be placed in a strange new world and then be confronted by a mob of poking, prodding humanity. So put off introducing your new puppy to your friends for a few days.

Hopefully you will be able to pick up your puppy yourself. When you pick up your Shih Tzu, find out from the breeder when its next feeding is, and how much food you should give it. While you are returning home, speak softly to your puppy, allowing it to become accustomed to the sound of your voice. From the first moment you have the puppy, you should begin calling it by its given name.

When you arrive home, take your puppy for a walk. It will probably want to urinate or defecate. Take it to the area that you have chosen to be its elimination area, and allow it to do its business. Give it plenty of time to relieve itself, for most puppies will want to explore for a while. After it is finished, be sure to pet and praise your puppy. You might as well start your outdoor puppy training right from the beginning. When all is done, it is time to go indoors.

Once inside, remove your puppy's leash, and allow it to explore your home undisturbed. Every five or ten minutes you can approach the puppy and speak to it. Feel free to pet it gently, but do not force the puppy to do what it does not want to do. In time, the sound of your footsteps and these brief approaches will quickly wear away any insecurity and ease the feeling of loneliness. After an hour or two, introduce your new puppy to the location of its food and water dishes (if it has not found them already) and feed it if necessary.

By the time you bring your Shih Tzu puppy home it should be fully weaned and able to feed on its own. When feeding your puppy, you will need to follow three fundamental rules. First, as already mentioned, feed your puppy the same type of food as the breeder used. Second, continue to follow the same feeding schedule as the breeder. Should the feeding times prove inconvenient, you can slowly change the meal times to suit your needs. Third, never bother your dog while it is eating or sleeping. Dogs that are surprised can act unpredictably and might snap at you. This is a very important rule to relay to your children.

After feeding the puppy, take it outside for another walk so it can relieve itself. On returning, let the puppy roam freely, but feel free to pet it and play with it. Once the puppy begins to tire, pick it up and place it in its sleeping box or cage. After a few days, your puppy will learn where its sleeping area is and when it is tired, will find its bed on its own.

The First Night

Chances are that the first night your puppy is in your home will not be pleasant for anyone concerned. You and your family will encounter your first real test of dog ownership, and it is of the utmost importance that you pass.

It is more than likely that on this first night your puppy will begin to whine, whimper, and wail, because it feels lonely and misses its mother and siblings. You must, however, not give in to the temptation of bringing the puppy to bed with you. You must remain firm. If you are using a cage, do not let the puppy out. If you do, the puppy will whine every time it wants to come out. If you use a sleeping box,

When lifting your puppy, place one hand under the puppy's hindquarters while using the other hand to support the chest and abdomen.

you might try to calm down the puppy by speaking softly, but do not take it from the box. No matter how hard you try, there will always be times when your Shih Tzu will be left alone. Your puppy must learn to deal with loneliness as soon as possible.

In order to ease some of the feelings of alienation and isolation, you can spend part of the first day accustoming your puppy to being left alone in the dark. Once your puppy seems comfortable in its new home, take one or two of the puppy's toys and place them in its cage or bed. Gently lift and place your puppy next to the toys. Then pull the shades or close the curtains, and turn out the lights in order to make the room as dark as possible. Then leave the room, making sure the puppy cannot get out and cannot hear or see you. If you are using a cage, you can lock the puppy in.

When you leave the puppy alone, it will probably cry and howl. If this happens, wait at least five minutes before returning. If the

puppy begins to settle down, wait at least ten minutes. If you repeat this procedure every half hour or so, it will be possible to prepare your puppy for the long and lonely night ahead.

If it is at all possible, do not leave your puppy alone for long periods of time for the first few days. If you must leave and there is no family member available, ask a neighbor or a close friend to puppy sit. Aside from the emotional stress being left alone can cause your puppy, the amount of trouble an unsupervised curious puppy can get into is mind-boggling.

Lifting and Carrying

Learning to lift and carry your Shih Tzu puppy properly can prevent the pain and possible injury that improper handling can cause. This is an important lesson for every member of your family to learn, and is really very easy. A healthy adult Shih Tzu will weigh only about 10 or 11 pounds (4.5–5.0 kg) so it can easily be lifted by most people in the same fashion as a puppy.

Place one hand under the puppy's chest and support the rump and hind legs with the other. That is all there is to it. This hold should give you a firm grip on your puppy, and make it difficult for it to squirm, which might cause

you to drop it. Never pick up your puppy by placing only one hand under its abdomen, and never grab the puppy by its legs. These methods can hurt the puppy. You should also forget that classic image of grabbing your puppy by the scruff of its neck. Besides being humiliating, it also hurts.

Shih Tzu and Children

While it may seem logical to get a toy dog such as a Shih Tzu for a young child, in reality this is not the best thing to do. This does not mean that in some instances children and Shih Tzu do not hit it off. It is just that Shih Tzu are not capable of withstanding the rough and tumble play that some children will dish out.

While Shih Tzu are naturally loving and affectionate, they may at times become intolerant of competing against children to gain your attention. Older children, however, and those who are more introspective, will more than likely form a lifetime relationship with a Shih Tzu. If you have an older, considerate child who would be willing to spend some time taking care of a Shih Tzu, there is no reason to believe that they cannot live in perfect harmony. However, if you have a more typical young child, you are well advised not to introduce a dog into your family that may not want to share the spotlight. If you do have young children and somehow come into possession of a Shih Tzu, you must instill in the youngsters the proper way to handle and play with the dog. It would also be good to get the children involved in the responsibilities of dog

When you bring your puppy home, allow it to check out its new environment.

Young children must be shown the proper way to handle a Shih Tzu.

ownership. Have your children feed, groom, and take your Shih Tzu for walks. In this way you can help build a bond between them that will lead to a long and lasting relationship.

Shih Tzu and Newborns

It can be quite difficult to convince a dog that it is no longer "God's gift" to your household once a new baby has arrived. This is doubly true for such a self-assured breed as the Shih Tzu. It is hard enough for a Shih Tzu to come into a family that already has very young children, but it will be much tougher if a Shih Tzu was there first. A well-established Shih Tzu will instinctively attempt to show dominance over this new arrival, and in doing so, establish a ranking order in which the baby is subordinate.

While some dogs may become very protective of the newborn, a Shih Tzu will more than likely try to compete with the baby for your attention. Be assured, however, that this type of situation will rarely cause your Shih Tzu to become aggressive toward the baby, but there is always a slight possibility of this happening.

If you already own a Shih Tzu and are expecting a new baby, there are certain precautions that you can take to assure your dog's acceptance of the newborn. Before the baby's birth, train your dog to sit or lie down for long periods of time. As the time increases, begin to perform other activities, preferably those you will be doing with your new baby. Make sure the dog acts properly while you go about these activities. Reward the dog for staying still and not attempting to follow you.

In order to familiarize your dog with the sights and sounds of a baby, you can invite friends, relatives, or neighbors who have infants to visit your home. In this case you are hoping that familiarity breeds contentment.

Try to make all changes in your house well before the baby arrives, so that the dog does not associate these radical changes with the baby. Make sure that the baby's furniture and supplies are in place several weeks before the baby is due. Any rearranging of furniture or decorating should also be done well in advance. Allow your Shih Tzu to adjust to all of these changes before it has to deal with the newcomer.

Once the dog has become accustomed to the changes, you can simulate all the activities that will occur after the baby is brought home. You might use a doll to imitate feeding, bathing, and changing the infant.

After the baby is born, give the dog something that the baby used in the hospital in order to familiarize it with the baby's scent. Upon returning home from the hospital, have the mother greet the dog without the baby being present. Then place the baby in the nursery and deny the dog access by using a folding gate or a screen door. In this way, the dog can see and hear the baby and get used to its presence before they actually meet.

When it is time to make the introduction, have one person control and reward the dog while another handles the baby. Have the dog sit and then show it the baby. Allow them to stay together for as long as the dog remains calm. Over the next couple of weeks you can gradually increase the length of time they spend together. Should the dog ever become overexcited or aggressive, you can confine it to a cage. However, this is not a permanent solution. If this type of behavior continues whenever they are together, you may want to seek the services of a professional dog handler. While this may be an unexpected expense, you can consider it money well spent.

Under no circumstances should you ever allow your dog to wander about unsupervised in the presence of the infant. On the other hand, never alienate your dog from the infant either. Allow the dog to be present during all the activities that involve the newborn. The more activities you allow them to share together, the stronger the bond that will form between your child and your Shih Tzu.

Canine Social Behavior

If you are considering owning more than one dog, or if you wish to understand why dogs react as they do to humans and each other, then you must examine their instinctive nature.

There are three major forms of social behavior that are considered instinctive (as opposed to social behavior that dogs have learned during their years of domestication). These are ranking order, territorial marking, and female scenting.

These instincts, which all dogs have, date back to a time when there was no bond between humans and dogs. They can easily be observed in the behavior of wild canines, like the wolf. Like wolves, the ancestors of our modern dogs were pack animals. They lived, bred, slept, and hunted in groups, understanding the need to remain together in order to survive. Naturally, when you get a group of individuals together, there are always going to be fights and disagreements. If this were to happen to one of us, we could simply leave or walk away. This would be fatal to wild dogs, who relied on helping each other track and hunt down food. Instead, these pack animals developed a system called ranking order.

Ranking order is a system that allowed wild dogs to coexist in a stable and, for the most part, peaceful environment. In this system, the dogs develop among themselves dominant-subordinate relationships in which the weaker animals give way to the stronger. Each dog's social ranking is largely determined by the animal's size, age, strength, and sex.

Ranking order is instinctive to all of our modern-day domesticated breeds. Whenever you put two dogs together, the first thing they will attempt to do is establish their ranking order. This usually takes place without trouble. Once established, it prevents fights between dogs in competition for food, living space, and breeding rights.

It is this social structure of dogs that allows humans to domesticate them. Once a human, as owner, establishes dominance over the subordinate dog, it will obey without resistance.

Another instinctive behavior that domestic dogs continue to exhibit is the marking of territories. While dogs will form ranking orders to prevent fights within a pack, they will also establish territories to prevent confrontations between two or more different packs. As dogs travel, they will urinate or defecate along their frequently traversed paths. These usually signify a border that a pack, or an individual in the case of your own dog, will attempt to defend.

The third instinctive behavior deals with the secretion of a scent by females that are in heat. In the wild, this behavior is crucial to the survival of the species. When a female secretes her scent, it signifies to all the males in the pack that she is ready to mate. The males, in turn, will challenge their ranking order with superiors. This ensues until a pack leader clearly shows his dominance, and wins the right to mate. Only the dominant male mates with the females in the pack. In the wild, only the strongest and healthiest pups survive. This mating with the dominant male gives the best chance of creating healthy puppies.

Female Dogs

If you own a female Shih Tzu, there are some special precautions you must take to prevent unwanted pregnancies. A female Shih Tzu will normally come into estrus (in heat, or in season) twice a year. Estrus refers to the period of time during which the female will accept mating with a male. This period will usually last about a week, but may last as long as two weeks. It is perfectly natural for a female to discharge blood during her season. To prevent staining to your rugs or furniture, you may want to confine her to a room that is easily cleaned. Sanitary napkins and diapers are also available for dogs in heat.

If you are considering breeding your female, you can find most of the information you will need in the chapter on Breeding Your Shih Tzu (see page 61). Should you choose not to breed her, then you will need to take steps to prevent your Shih Tzu from becoming pregnant. One option is to have your dog spayed. Spaying is the only sure-fire way of preventing an unwanted litter. Spaying also has many other benefits. As mentioned earlier, a spayed female is much less likely to suffer from such ailments as breast tumors, false pregnancies, and ovarian cysts. Just remember that this procedure is permanent. Once your female is spayed, she can *never* have puppies, so you must be absolutely sure about your decision.

Should you decide not to have your dog spayed, there are other ways to prevent her from becoming pregnant until you are ready. The objective, of course, would be to prevent your female from coming into contact with all male dogs. This is not as easy as it sounds. As previously mentioned, during this time your female dog will secrete a scent that will attract male dogs from far and wide to your doorstep. These stray male dogs may camp outside your house and hide out of sight, just waiting for the right opportunity. If all this is not bad enough, you must also deal with your female, who will also be undergoing some attitude changes during this time. Her mating urges might be so strong that she does not heed your commands, especially if she knows that there is a male dog nearby. As you can see, there are numerous forces working against you.

For this reason, you must never let your female go outside alone during the estrus period. Even a completely fenced-in yard may not protect her. Some male dogs with a very strong urge to mate are capable of scaling a 6-foot (1.8-m) fence with ease. You will also have to worry about your female (or smaller male dogs) burrowing under the fence, or squeezing through a small gap in the fence.

Your veterinarian may also be able to help you take additional precautions. Because a spayed show dog would be disqualified from bench competition, some of their owners have their veterinarians administer estrus-control medication. These medications also prevent her from upsetting the male competition. You should be aware, however, that these medications may have some side effects. Discuss them at length with your veterinarian before deciding if you will use them. Chlorophyll tablets are also available through your veterinarian. These tablets will help neutralize the odor of your dog's secretions; however, they will not prevent her from becoming pregnant.

Vacation Time

Vacationing with your Shih Tzu can be a fun and rewarding experience for both of you. All it takes is a little advance planning. Transporting animals is performed quite frequently by almost all companies in the travel business in the United States. All major airlines accept dogs. Some will even supply a large crate to house your Shih Tzu during the trip. Your Shih Tzu, however, will not be able to travel in the seat next to you. Usually all animals are placed in the pressurized cabins of the luggage department. Be sure to check all the rules and costs of transporting your pet well in advance.

All major railways in the United States also have accommodations for the traveling canine. Most will only transport dogs if they travel in a shipping crate in the baggage car. Some railways will even supply the crate. Call the railroad for costs and regulations.

If you are traveling by car, you can place your Shih Tzu in its cage. Do not allow the dog to run free in the car. There are usually enough problems on the road to deal with; you don't need the additional worry about what your Shih Tzu is doing. When driving, open the window enough to give your dog fresh air, but do not expose it to drafts. Drafts can lead to ear, eye, and throat ailments. Make rest stops about every two hours. During these breaks, take the dog for a walk

In order for multiple dogs to coexist in your household, you should understand their nature.

If you do not breed your female, you should seriously consider having her spayed

and allow it to relieve itself. Needless to say, walk the dog on a leash. You should also give your dog a drink of cool water. It can get very hot inside a car, and frequent drinks will help to prevent dehydration.

Many young dogs may become carsick if they are not used to traveling. Your veterinarian can supply you with motion-sickness tablets to prevent this.

If you are traveling abroad, you should familiarize yourself with any laws in the countries you will visit that pertain to dogs. You can obtain a copy of the laws by writing or visiting the consulate of these countries. While most countries have minimal requirements concerning dogs, some have special quarantine regulations. To visit most foreign countries your dog will require a valid health certificate, which you can get from a licensed veterinarian. You will also need a current certificate of vaccination against rabies (less than six months old).

When you pack your dog's suitcase, remember to bring the following items: food and water dishes, collar, leash, muzzle, cage with blanket, and grooming equipment. If it is at all possible, bring enough of your dog's regular canned and/or dry food to last the entire trip.

Boarding

If you cannot find any reliable neighbor, friend, or family member willing to dog sit, then you must consider boarding your Shih Tzu. Start by contacting the breeder from whom you purchased your dog. If it is not possible to leave your dog with the breeder, then you may decide to use a boarding kennel.

Before leaving your dog at a boarding kennel, you should inspect the facilities thoroughly. Make sure they are clean and that the operating staff is knowledgeable. An adult Shih Tzu should have little problem adjusting to a temporary change in its environment. If it can be avoided, however, a Shih Tzu puppy should never be left alone or at a boarding kennel for a long period of time.

If you brush your dog daily, it should only take a few minutes. Aside from this, your Shih Tzu will only require additional grooming periodically.

To make the grooming easier, I recommend acclimating your dog to these sessions while it is still a puppy.

Equipment

To keep your Shih Tzu in top show condition, you will need the following equipment: a stiff bristle brush, a slicker brush, a comb, scissors, and nail clippers designed for dogs. Another handy item is a tangle-removing spray, formulated for dogs.

Regardless of how experienced you become at grooming your Shih Tzu, you should always have a small bottle of

Pay special attention to the coat under your Shih Tzu's front legs. This is an area where matting can quickly occur if it is not brushed frequently enough.

styptic powder on hand in case of accidents that result in bleeding.

Coat Care

A Shih Tzu's coat is much easier to brush if misted with water or tangle remover. After you dampen the coat, you can brush it until it is dry, then apply more spray if needed. Light daily brushings and a thorough weekly brushing will prevent unmanageable matting.

When brushing, begin with the chest, underside, and inner legs. Place the dog on its back, spray the exposed coat, and brush lightly with a bristle brush. Make a part in the dog's coat and brush it in layers, starting at the skin and stroking toward the tips. When you are done with the stomach and chest, use the slicker brush to fluff up the coat around the feet and legs.

Turn the dog onto each side so you can do the heavy coat on the side of the hocks and body. Again spray, part the hairs, and brush in layers from the skin to the tips. Once all is completed, the dog should be allowed to lie right side up. Spray, and then part its coat down the middle from the nose to the base of the tail. Brush the long outer coat and then comb it out until smooth;

then spray and brush out the dog's tail. The final step is to carefully smooth out the dog's whiskers and the hair around the face and eyes using a fine-tooth comb.

Part of your normal routine should be to trim any excess hair between the dog's toes as short as possible. This can help reduce the chance of infection in bad weather and can improve traction. If you do encounter severe matting, try using a commercial coat oil. These oils can be applied to the matted hair to make combing much easier.

If you wish, you can tie up the hair on the top of the Shih Tzu's head. Once the grooming session is over, reward your dog with a kind word, some affectionate petting, and a few minutes of play.

Always look for signs of parasites when grooming your dog. If you see signs of fleas or ticks, address the problem immediately. Contact your veterinarian if you notice anything unusual.

Bathing

Unless your dog smells bad, is totally filthy, has gotten covered with something greasy, or is about to be entered into a dog show, you should not bathe your dog. Unlike human skin, a dog's skin is full of oil glands, which help keep the skin soft and prevent it from becoming dry and cracked. They also secrete an oil that helps the dog's coat repel water. Excessive use of any soap or shampoo will remove the oil produced by these glands and dry out the skin or cause excessive shedding.

When a bath is absolutely necessary, you should start by brushing your dog to remove tangles. Use a high-quality shampoo designed especially for dogs, and avoid getting shampoo or water in your dog's ears or eyes. After shampooing, thoroughly rinse out the coat. When the bath is finished, gently pat the dog dry with a towel. Let your pet shake several times, and then wrap it in a towel and blot dry. Then comb and part the dog's hair. Keep the dog indoors during the drying process.

Ear and Eye Care

During your thorough weekly grooming session, give special attention to your Shih Tzu's ears. Use a commercial ear-cleaning solution to carefully remove any wax build-up. To clean the ear, hold it open with one hand and gently clean the inside of the flap with a cotton ball dipped in cleaning solution. Use a fresh cotton ball for each ear. You can clean the outermost portions of the ear canal using a cotton swab that has been dipped in the solution.

Also, inspect your Shih Tzu's eyes regularly to ensure they are free of discharge. Use a moistened cotton ball to remove any dirt around your dog's eyes. Again, use a fresh cotton ball for each eye. If you notice any damage or inflammation, contact your veterinarian.

Nail and Paw Care

Learn how to use a pair of clippers before you trim your dog's nails. An experienced dog groomer or veterinarian can show you how to

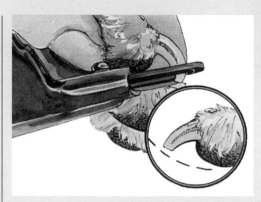

When trimming your Shih Tzu's nails, be sure to clip them at an angle. Be careful not to cut the sensitive quick.

use them. The center of the dog's nail is called the quick, and it contains the blood vessels and nerve endings. You can see them when you examine the dog's nails (it is normally a pink to deeper red color). If you cut the quick, you will cause the dog much pain. In addition, the quick grows out as the nail lengthens. If you wait too long between pedicures, you may have to cut the quick to get the nail back to a comfortable length. Always cut the nail as close to the quick as possible, and be sure to hold your pet's paw firmly but gently.

Tooth Care

Tooth care begins with feeding your dog plenty of hard foods, such as dog biscuits and rawhide bones, to slow down the accumulation of tartar. Excessive tartar can lead to gum deterioration and tooth loss. You should also brush your dog's teeth once a week with a commercial toothpaste that is formulated specifically for dogs. Before brushing, inspect the dog's teeth and gums for signs of infection and tartar buildup. Excessive tartar can be scraped off by your veterinarian.

NUTRITION

Understanding Nutrition

Dogs, like all members of the canine family, have been scientifically classified as carnivores. They can, however, utilize a wide variety of foodstuffs, including fruits and vegetables. One is therefore able to provide a dog with its daily nutritional requirements in numerous ways.

All foods are composed of one or more of the seven nutrient groups. These groups—proteins, fats, carbohydrates, vitamins, minerals, trace elements, and water—are all essential for the proper growth and metabolism of a dog. And these nutrients must be supplied in the correct proportions if your dog is to be able to utilize them properly.

The type and quantity of nutrients a dog needs depends on several factors. Individual growth rates, exercise, rate of metabolism, age, and many environmental factors will all influence the quantity and quality of the food your Shih Tzu requires. As you can guess, the nutritional requirements of your dog will change several times during the course of its lifetime.

Importance of Water

Water is an extremely important part of your Shih Tzu's diet because it is vital to all living cells. Your Shih Tzu's body is comprised of

Commercial diets cater to every stage of your dog's life.

about 60 percent water. Unlike some animals, dogs do not have the ability to store large quantities of water. Therefore, in order to replace any water loss, your Shih Tzu must always have a readily available source of water. Your dog's water intake will depend on several factors, including air temperature, type of food it eats, the amount of exercise it gets, and its temperament. If your dog's water dish is not always left on the floor, then you should offer it water at least three times a day. The water you give your dog should be cool, not cold.

What to Feed

Since the turn of the century, our understanding of animal nutrition and our ability to utilize our knowledge have enabled scientists to provide our pets with extremely healthy foods. In fact, you can purchase several different types of commercial dog foods that have been specially formulated to provide your Shih Tzu with virtually every essential nutrient, while meeting its energy needs at the same time.

Commercial dog foods offer many advantages over preparing your Shih Tzu's meals from scratch, the most obvious advantage being the ease of preparation. However, perhaps the most important advantage is that a top-quality, well-balanced commercial dog food can give your pet 100 percent of its nutritional and energy needs. Because you choose to use a commercial

The Basic Nutrient Groups

Nutrient (Sources)	Nutritional Value and Symptoms of Deficiencies
Protein (meat, eggs, fish, milk, soybean meal, brewer's yeast, wheat germ)	Provides energy and amino acids essential for growth, development, maintenance of strong bones, and muscles; promotes production of antibodies, enzymes, and hormones; deficiencies include poor growth, weight loss, loss of appetite, and poor hair and coat.
Fats (meat, vegetable oils)	Provide source of energy and heat; supply essential fatty acids, fat soluble vitamins (A, D, E, and K); make food more palatable; necessary for proper development of skin and coat; deficiencies include dry and coarse coat and skin lesions.
Carbohydrates (sugars, starches)	Help regulate energy balance; supply fiber and roughage to help regulate digestive system and help prevent diarrhea/constipation.
Vitamins (brewer's yeast, vegetables, fruits, cod liver oil, wheat germ oil)	Prevent numerous illnesses and diseases; help regulate many bodily functions including growth, muscle development, and fertility; deficiencies can lead to skin lesions, depression, conjunctivitis, nervous disorders, rickets, and osteoporosis (as well as numerous other disorders).
Minerals/Trace Minerals (bones, meat, grains, fruit, vegetables)	Prevent numerous ailments and diseases; help regulate many bodily functions including bone formation; help regulate water balance within a dog's body. (Trace minerals are named because they are required in very small quantities.)

dog food for your pet does not mean that you love it any less than if you were to cook its meals from scratch. In fact, try thinking of using a high-quality commercial dog food as a way to maximize your dog's health and longevity. The advice of your veterinarian or breeder can be invaluable when choosing which commercial dog food is right for your dog.

Although you might think that your devoted pet is a real member of your family, you are better off not feeding it like one. Trying to prepare your dog's diet from scratch can be very difficult and time-consuming, but you also run the risk of leaving out an important nutrient that could eventually lead to health problems.

Commercial Dog Foods

There are basically three different types of commercial dog food available. They are dry, semimoist, and moist. Many times the choice of which type you use depends on which one your Shih Tzu will accept and eat. Each type is formulated using different ingredients, and there will also be changes from brand to brand. Be sure to read the labels carefully for nutritional information and feeding tips.

Dry foods come in pellets, kibbles, extruded products, or whole biscuits. These foods, as the name implies, are low in moisture (10–12 percent). They contain mostly grains, cereal by-products, soybean, animal-meat meals, milk products, and fats as well as vitamins and minerals. These foods can be moistened with water prior to feeding.

Semimoist dog foods are higher in moisture (usually 25–30 percent). These foods contain the same ingredients as the dry varieties do, but usually have less meat meals and more whole meat. Because of the high moisture, these nonrefrigerated formulas have extra preservatives added to them to guard against spoilage. Semimoist foods are usually shaped into patties or simulated meat chunks.

Canned dog foods are usually very high in moisture (about 70–75 percent). They also come in several varieties, including all meat, meat, dinners, or flavored. Except for all meat, which contains 100 percent meat products, most forms of canned dog foods are balanced and nutritionally complete. Be sure to check the information on the labels. Those that are not 100 percent complete are designed to be added to dry foods to make them more appealing.

Choosing a type of commercial dog food may be confusing because there are so many successful formulas, and many of them differ greatly in their ingredients. As I have previously mentioned, your Shih Tzu itself may be the deciding factor. You can have the most perfect nutritionally complete meal available, but if your dog refuses to eat it, what good does it do? For the most part, Shih Tzu will eat most foods without any problems. However, this breed of dog does have its share of finicky eaters.

Important note: Once you have found a food that your Shih Tzu seems to enjoy, it is best to stick with it and resist the temptation to try a new brand. Changing your dog's diet can cause numerous digestive problems such as diarrhea or constipation. If you give your dog a high-quality, well-balanced diet, it will thrive on it for as long as its nutritional requirements remain the same. Do not worry, a dog will not become bored with the same old thing. If your Shih Tzu should refuse its diet, this is an indication that something is wrong either emotionally or physically. It may actually be no more than a mild stomach upset. However, if the dog should refuse to eat for a day or two, take it to a veterinarian. In many cases, early diagnosis is the key to curing the ailment.

Feeding by Age

The advances in animal nutrition combined with our increased knowledge of animal health have brought about the emergence of a completely new concept in commercial dog foods. You can now find specialized dog foods designed to supply complete nutrition during every phase of your dog's life. In addition to puppy foods, you can now find special diets for active dogs, inactive and overweight dogs, and older dogs. There are even specialized diets made for dogs with medical problems such as heart conditions and kidney disorders. It is possible to find a commercial food for each phase of your dog's development. In addition to purchasing a different quality food for every

The older your dog gets, the less food it will need to maintain a proper diet.

phase of your dog's life, there are other ways of supplying your dog with the added nutrients it may need. The following is a summary of your Shih Tzu's needs during certain periods of its life, as well as some suggestions on how to fulfill its requirements.

Puppies Under Five Months Old

For the first four to five weeks of a puppy's life, all of the nourishment needed is obtained from its mother. Once the puppy is weaned, it is the responsibility of

Your growing puppy will require a lot of nutrients.

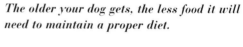

Water is very important for your dog; make sure it always has an available supply.

its owner to feed it properly. The body of a puppy in this age group is constantly changing. Its body is growing and the development of the internal structure is extremely rapid. Therefore, your puppy requires about twice the nutrients per pound of body weight as a mature adult dog. High-quality commercial puppy foods are formulated to meet these needs.

Your Shih Tzu puppy should eat the equivalent of 5 to 10 percent of its body weight per day. Divide this amount of food into three feedings per day using the same feeding schedule as the breeder. Any changes you make in your puppy's diet, or in the scheduled feeding times, should be made slowly so as not to disturb its delicate digestive system.

Always serve your puppy's food at room temperature, and always keep a supply of fresh, clean water in your puppy's dish. Your puppy's water should be cool, but not too cold. This is especially important during the winter, for cold water can give the puppy chills. Thoroughly wash the food and water dishes every day. This will help prevent the growth of harmful bacteria.

At 14 weeks of age, your puppy's permanent teeth will begin pushing through the gums, causing extreme discomfort and pain. To ease this discomfort, give the puppy a rawhide bone, or a manageable-sized hard beef bone to gnaw on. If your puppy does not get a bone to gnaw on, you can be assured it will find something else to chew in order to relieve the pain. Because Shih Tzu do seem to have expensive taste, they usually gnaw only on the finest furniture and imported leather. Rawhide bones are the least costly alternative.

Puppies Five to Seven Months Old

When your Shih Tzu puppy reaches this age, it does not need to eat as frequently, so reduce the feedings to twice a day. You can monitor the puppy's food intake by watching its weight. Should it become too heavy, decrease the amount of food you give it. However, because your puppy is still growing, you will more than likely have to increase its intake. Vitamin and mineral supplements can be added to the puppy's food, as per your veterinarian's recommendations.

Puppies Seven to Ten Months Old

Your Shih Tzu is now beginning to reach full maturity, and its growth rate will begin to decrease. Your Shih Tzu will therefore require less food. Continue to give the dog two meals daily, only make the portions smaller. At this point you should consider getting a commercial diet for older puppies. These diets will give your puppy the nutrients it requires, and will help ease the transition of switching your dog's puppy-growth food for its adult maintenance diet.

Adult Dogs

By now your dog has reached full maturity and it no longer needs a diet formulated for growing puppies. Instead, your dog requires a high-quality maintenance food. Once you have selected a quality diet, you can observe its effects by monitoring your Shih Tzu's coat condition and physical activity. A proper diet will produce a smooth, soft, and shiny coat. Improperly fed dogs have dull, coarse coats, and quickly become lethargic and fatigued.

How much food your Shih Tzu should be fed will depend primarily upon its weight and the amount of exercise it receives, although temperament, age, sex, and weather conditions may also affect food consumption. The best way to monitor how much food your Shih Tzu needs is to weigh it every few weeks. If your dog is gaining weight, reduce the amount of food it receives and give it more exercise.

Older Dogs

Over the past 20 years, there has been a steady increase in the geriatric portion of the canine population in the United States. The increase in the average life expectancy of dogs is mainly due to advances in preventive medicine and a better understanding of canine nutrition. Recent studies indicate that older dogs, like puppies, require a diet higher in protein and lower in fat.

Research shows that older dogs lose their ability to utilize fat as a source of energy. So instead of using it, the older dog stores it, thus becoming overweight. To make up for this lost source of energy, the older dog requires a diet higher in protein. Once again, commercial dog foods are available that are designed to meet the nutritional needs of the older dog.

Care should be taken when feeding the geriatric dog that has shown signs of kidney problems. While it has not been proven, some experts feel that excess protein in the geriatric diet will put an increased workload on a dog's kidneys. Caution must therefore be taken when feeding an elderly pet. While there are several commercial diets that cater to the older dog, it would be prudent for you to consult with your veterinarian before making a choice.

AILMENTS AND ILLNESSES

In General

While this chapter is dedicated to the description, symptoms, and remedies of canine illnesses, there is no need to become overly alarmed. The descriptions of the ailments, while sometimes graphic, are not meant to scare you or send you running to the veterinarian every time your dog scratches its ears.

In fact, most ailments can be avoided by using preventive medicine and by feeding your Shih Tzu a healthy, well-balanced diet. With proper feeding, and keeping to scheduled visits to the veterinarian for booster shots and routine examinations, you can help your Shih Tzu avoid many medical problems. By combining these measures with proper hygiene and an adequate exercise program, you will have done everything possible to assure that your Shih Tzu lives a long and healthy life.

Dogs that are neglected and do not receive adequate care, however, run a much greater risk of encountering one or more of these diseases or ailments. So while the descriptions of these illnesses are not meant to frighten, if it does convince just one dog owner to take better care of a neglected dog, I will consider this book a success.

Your Shih Tzu should have routine veterinarian's examinations throughout its life.

Understanding Symptoms

In medical terms, a symptom is defined as a phenomenon that arises from and accompanies a particular disease or disorder, and serves as an indicator of it. While symptoms do indicate that your Shih Tzu is not feeling well, they may not necessarily be a sign of a serious illness. In addition, a single abnormal symptom, or a combination of them, may not always point to a specific illness. Understanding the symptoms associated with certain ailments may help narrow down the possible cause, and it usually takes the extensive training of a veterinarian to discover the exact nature of the illness.

There are certain symptoms your Shih Tzu may exhibit when it is not feeling well that you, as the dog's owner, should be able to recognize quickly. Watch for loss of appetite or thirst, excessive appetite or thirst, physical exhaustion, poor coat condition, excessive coughing or sneezing, frequent wheezing or runny nose, pale gums, foul breath, repeated vomiting, slight paralysis or limping, trembling or shaking, sudden weight loss, any swelling or lumps on the body, cloudy or orange-colored urine, inability to urinate, uncontrolled urination, diarrhea, moaning or whimpering, discharge from the eyes, and any unusual slobbering or salivation. If you notice any one or a combination of these symptoms, you should call your veterinarian. Many diseases can cause severe damage if not treated promptly, and in many cases, early diagnosis of an ailment is the key to its cure.

Two of the most common symptoms of illness are vomiting and diarrhea. Both can occur frequently in dogs. However, they do not always indicate the presence of a serious ailment. Therefore they warrant further discussion.

Vomiting

Vomiting does not always indicate a problem, especially when you are dealing with the mother of newborn puppies. A recent mother may instinctively regurgitate food in an attempt to feed her puppies. In addition, young dogs, especially puppies, often devour their food so greedily that their natural defense mechanisms send the food back up again. This unpleasant behavior usually disappears as the dog matures. Extremely nervous dogs may also regurgitate food whenever something bothers them or if they become frightened. Sometimes dogs will intentionally eat some grasses to force themselves to vomit. They may do this simply to purge their digestive system. However, sometimes it may indicate a larger problem.

Vomiting should only be considered significant when it occurs persistently. Internal parasites, infections, and several digestive disorders and diseases can cause your dog to vomit frequently. Persistent vomiting is usually accompanied by irregular bowel movements, such as diarrhea. Dogs that exhibit these symptoms should get veterinary attention.

Diarrhea

An occasional soft stool is nothing for you to worry about, although diarrhea may follow. During the warmer months your dog may drink a lot more water in order to cool down and prevent dehydration. This increased water intake may cause loose stool or diarrhea, which usually clears up rapidly. Continued watery bowel movements, on the other hand, indicate a serious ailment. Diarrhea is a symptom of nearly every canine ailment including worms, distemper, and poisoning, and can even be brought about by nervous disorders.

If diarrhea occurs infrequently, and your dog seems otherwise healthy, it may be caused by nothing more than a minor stomach upset. Should your Shih Tzu suffer from an occasional attack of diarrhea and you suspect its diet may be the cause, ask your veterinarian to give his or her recommendation regarding the diet most likely to agree with your dog's digestive system. Also, during these times, be sure your dog's water dish is always full of clean, cool water. If the diarrhea persists for several days, take the dog to the veterinarian. If left untreated, severe diarrhea can cause dehydration. If at any time you see blood in your dog's stool, contact your veterinarian immediately.

Preventive Medicine

Prevention starts by feeding your Shih Tzu a well-balanced diet. Proper hygiene and an adequate exercise program are equally important to the physical well-being of your dog. Your dog's mental health depends largely on having a happy relationship with its master. These elements should all be part of your dog's daily routine. One form of preventive medicine, however, which you cannot give your dog are vaccinations and booster shots against infectious diseases. For these you must take your Shih Tzu to the veterinarian. These, however, are no less important when it comes to preventing your dog from becoming ill.

Vaccinations

Dogs are vaccinated in order to prevent them from contracting and spreading infectious diseases. Prior to the discovery of vaccines, several infectious diseases ran rampant throughout the canine population causing numerous fatalities. These diseases were usually caused by either bacteria or viruses. Thanks to the dedicated work of many researchers, there is now a vaccine to immunize your pet against all the major infectious diseases. While these vaccines are extremely effective, some do not guarantee permanent protection. In these cases, your dog may require booster shots at regular intervals. It will take three or four weeks for the first group of immunizations to become completely effective. So keep your newly vaccinated puppy away from all nonimmunized dogs until the vaccines can take full effect.

A quality breeder will have his or her Shih Tzu puppies vaccinated before selling them, and will supply you with a copy of the dog's medical records, indicating the dates of treatment. These records will remind you when your dog needs booster shots. There are six infectious diseases for which your dog will require immunization. These are rabies, canine distemper, canine hepatitis, leptospirosis, parainfluenza, and parvovirus.

Rabies is considered the most dangerous known dog disease. This viral infection attacks the dog's nervous system, and can be transmitted to all warm-blooded animals, including humans. The usual method of transmission is through a bite in which the infected saliva of a rabid animal enters the victim's body. The disease can also be contracted if the saliva comes into contact with an open wound.

Early symptoms of rabies include rapid behavioral changes. An infected dog may act very friendly one minute, and extremely irritable the next. Later symptoms include a loss of appetite, frequent urination, and attempts to bite or eat foreign objects, such as wood or stones. The dog then becomes vicious and suffers paralysis of the face and throat, which causes the dog to drool excessively, and is complicated by an inability to swallow. Finally the dog becomes more paralyzed, cannot eat or drink, and dies shortly thereafter.

The rabies vaccine will not save an unvaccinated dog that is bitten and infected by a rabid animal; therefore all dogs need to be immunized against the disease. To maintain your pet's immunity, it must be given a booster shot every three years. Due to the fact that this disease can be transmitted to humans, all rabies incidents are considered a public health hazard and should be reported. If you suspect any stray dog or other animal in your neighborhood of having rabies, you should report this to the public-health authorities immediately.

Canine distemper was once second to rabies in respect to its danger to dogs. Today, however, dogs that are vaccinated against this disease will not contract it easily. Canine distemper is a highly contagious viral disease that is spread through the urine, feces, saliva, and even nasal discharge of the infected animal. The virus may also be carried on blankets, brushes, and clothing.

The early stages of this disease are characterized by fever, diarrhea, depression, a dry cough, and watery discharge from the eyes and nose. Advanced symptoms may include a loss

of equilibrium, cramps, twitching of leg and facial muscles, convulsive seizures, and partial paralysis.

Canine distemper is almost always fatal to a young dog that has not been immunized. In older dogs the disease can cause damage to the central nervous system. If a puppy's mother was properly vaccinated, she is able to passively immunize the puppy by passing antibodies (proteins that attack diseases) to her young through her milk. Such immunization lasts throughout the nursing period. After weaning, the puppies will need additional vaccinations. Once a dog contracts canine distemper, it can be very difficult to treat. Thus the only effective protection against canine distemper is vaccination and booster shots.

Canine hepatitis should not be confused with human hepatitis. Canine hepatitis is a contagious viral disease that primarily attacks the liver and gastrointestinal tract. This disease is spread

Vaccinations will help guard against infectious diseases.

throughout the canine population in much the same way as canine distemper. Canine hepatitis cannot be contracted by humans; however, they can carry the virus on their clothing. Dogs that have been vaccinated against this disease rarely contract it. However, it is almost always fatal to unvaccinated puppies. Older dogs that contract the disease can sometimes be saved.

Symptoms of canine hepatitis include diarrhea, fever, severe thirst, lethargy, inflammation of the nasal passages, and liver inflammation, which makes the abdomen sensitive to the touch. In order to relieve the pain in their liver and stomach, dogs with canine hepatitis may arch their backs and rub their bellies on the floor. This disease develops extremely rapidly. Affected dogs may appear healthy one day, and very ill the next.

Parvovirus began to appear in dogs only in the last two decades, and two forms of the disease are now known. One type causes an inflammation of the heart muscles of very young puppies. Infected animals quickly collapse and die of heart complications. The other, more common form, is called parvoviral enteritis. It is characterized by constant vomiting of a foamy yellow-brown liquid and bloody, foul-smelling diarrhea. Both of these result in heavy fluid loss that can lead to dehydration and death in a few days. Patting the undersides of an infected dog will cause it to wince in pain. Parvoviral enteritis can occur in dogs of all ages. Both forms of the virus are carried and transmitted much the same way as canine distemper.

Puppies should be vaccinated against parvovirus before their fourteenth week. Immunization against the virus must be repeated frequently in order to be effective. Yearly booster shots are recommended. If the disease is detected early enough, an unvaccinated dog can sometimes be saved through lengthy, painful, and expensive treatments. Clearly, immunization is by far the best way to protect your Shih Tzu.

Parainfluenza or Kennel cough refers to viral and/or bacterial infections that affect the upper respiratory tract of dogs. The disease agents, which cause an inflammation of the trachea and bronchi, are common whenever and wherever dogs congregate. If you are planning to board your dog in a kennel, be sure it is vaccinated against these diseases. Yearly booster shots are recommended.

Leptospirosis is caused by bacteria transmitted through the urine of rats, mice, or infected dogs. Dogs can only contract the disease through ingestion. Leptospirosis attacks an infected dog's liver and kidneys.

The symptoms of this disease may be very similar to those of canine distemper and canine hepatitis. However, leptospirosis usually causes a kidney infection that changes the color and odor of the urine. The urine of an infected dog often has a deep yellow to orange color, and has a strong offensive odor.

On very rare occasions, leptospirosis can be transmitted to humans. Vaccinations against this disease are the only way to protect your dog, yourself, and your family. Leptospirosis causes a dog a great deal of pain, and if not treated in its early stages, is almost always fatal.

Vaccination Schedule

Temporary immunizations: Starting at four to six weeks of age, the passive immunity that a puppy receives from its mother's milk begins to wear off. At this point you must take your puppy to the veterinarian for its vaccinations. Your veterinarian will administer a series of immunizations to guard against distemper, canine hepatitis, parvovirus, kennel cough, and leptospirosis. Then you will have to return every three or four weeks until the puppy is four months old so that it can receive the necessary booster shots. Anti-rabies vaccinations are usually not given until the puppy reaches the age of four months.

Booster shots: By having your Shih Tzu immunized regularly, you are providing it with maximum protection against the various infectious diseases discussed above. Your veterinarian will explain the frequency of each type of booster. Whenever you bring your Shih Tzu to the veterinarian for its booster shots, bring a sample of its stool in a plastic bag so that it can be checked for infestations.

Prior to mating: A female Shih Tzu that is to be bred should be brought to the veterinarian prior to her season. It is important for her to receive booster shots so that she can adequately supply her puppies with the passive immunity they need. You should also bring a stool sample so that she can be checked for worms and treated if necessary.

Internal Parasites

Roundworms are considered the most common internal parasites found in the canine population. They are white, cylindrical in shape, and can grow up to 4 inches (10 cm) long. The adult roundworms live in a dog's intestinal tract, where they will imbed themselves. The adults then lay eggs, which are passed out within the dog's stool. If the eggs are ingested

by another animal, they will grow into adults within their new host, thus continuing the cycle. Roundworms rarely cause serious illness in adult dogs. However, a heavy infestation can be fatal to a puppy. Roundworms are frequently passed from a pregnant mother to her puppies. So be sure to have your female's stool checked, and have her wormed, if necessary, prior to mating her.

Symptoms of roundworm infestation include diarrhea, cramps, irregular appetite, weakness, bloated belly, and in severe cases, paralysis. In addition, the infested dog's anus may itch, in which case the dog will squat down and skid its rump across the floor in an attempt to relieve the itch.

Tapeworms also live in a dog's intestinal tract. They can be found in young and old dogs alike. The most common source of tapeworm is fleas, which act as carriers of the worm's eggs. When the flea is ingested by a biting dog, the eggs can begin to grow in its intestines. Tapeworm eggs can also be found in uncooked meats such as pork or lamb; however, this is extremely uncommon.

The head of this worm has a series of hooks and suckers that it uses to attach itself tenaciously to the dog's small intestine. The worm will feed upon material that the host is attempting to digest. The body of the tapeworm grows in a long segmented chain, with the tail section containing many eggs. On occasion, the worm will release the egg-containing section, which will be passed in

The life cycle of the tapeworm: Eggs are carried by fleas and ingested by the dog; eggs grow into segmented adults that make more eggs.

the dog's stool. These segments look like grains of rice and often stick to the hairs surrounding the dog's anus.

The symptoms of tapeworm infestation may take a long time to develop. The best way to diagnose a tapeworm problem is by having the stool checked. Your veterinarian will treat tapeworms with a medication that is specifically designed for this ailment.

Heartworm is a parasite transmitted by mosquitoes that carry the worm larvae. Because of this, heartworms are only prevalent in certain areas. When a dog is bitten by these mosquitoes, the larvae can enter the bloodstream. They live within the lumen of the organs they infest (primarily the heart and lungs). They cause the heart to work harder, age rapidly, and eventually weaken. It takes about six months for the larvae to develop into adult heartworms.

Two drugs are presently used to prevent and treat heartworm: Ivermectin and Milbemycin Oximine. Both medications are administered once a month and are effective for up to 45 days. If you forget to give your Shih Tzu its medication on the designated day of the month, you have about 15 additional days to remember to administer it, and the dog is still protected. Unlike previously used daily heartworm medications, Ivermectin and Milbemycin Oximine will not further hurt the dog that is already infested. Both drugs are available from your veterinarian.

Treating a dog that already has heartworm is difficult and can be costly, whereas preventing them is easy and costs significantly less. If you live in an area where heartworms are known to occur, have your dog tested, and consult your veterinarian on the administration of a heartworm preventative.

Other internal parasites include hookworms, kidney worms, lung worms, and whipworms. Infestations by each type of worm will exhibit different symptoms and require specific medications. To make treatment totally effective, you should contact your veterinarian if you suspect that your Shih Tzu is infected. Inexperienced owners can do more harm than good for their dog when they begin experimenting with worming medications, which are after all a form of poison.

External Parasites

Fleas are by far the most common of all parasites that affect dogs. Fleas are small, wingless, bloodsucking external parasites that cause more suffering to dogs than any other ailment. The fact that fleas are wingless, however, does not mean that they lack mobility. Fleas are world-class jumpers and they will commonly jump several feet from one dog to another. Fleas will irritate the dog with their constant biting. When they bite, they secrete certain toxic and allergenic compounds, which will result in your dog scratching and biting. Some dogs that are hypersensitive to these secretions will scratch and bite almost to the point of self-mutilation. Many times an excessive amount of biting and licking will produce other skin problems such as eczema or a patch of dermatitis (hot spot). These patches are most commonly seen on the rump or thigh, and are usually treated with an antibiotic ointment (available from your veterinarian).

Fleas can enter your home, even if your Shih Tzu does not venture outside. They can hop in from outside or even hitch a ride on a human. Unfortunately, once you get fleas in your home, they are often very difficult to eliminate, especially because the larvae can remain dormant for an astonishingly long time and can withstand severe environmental conditions.

The life cycle of the flea, from egg to larvae to adult, is between three and six weeks. To eliminate fleas in your house, you must break this cycle. This means that you will have to repeat your initial efforts in several weeks to get the eggs and larvae that were not destroyed the first time around, which will by that time be new adults.

You can check your dog for fleas by parting its coat, exposing skin, and looking for the following signs; bits of brown dust, which when wiped with a wet paper towel dissolve into a red liquid (digested blood excreted by fleas) and reddened skin. If you see small, fast-moving brown shapes, they are probably fleas. You should also check your dog's bedding for the presence of flea dust or fleas.

Believe it or not, the primary flea that infests dogs in North America and large areas of Europe is the cat flea. Under normal conditions, this flea spends most of its adult life on the host animal, where it lays its eggs. Some eggs will fall off the dog, and therefore can be found wherever your pets spend time, such as in their bedding, in carpets, or in the yard.

Several methods are available to kill or discourage fleas, including collars, shampoos, dips, room and yard sprays, foggers, and powders. To complicate matters even more, most of these contain a variety of natural or synthetic pesticides, or sometimes both. Some have residual properties, which means that they are formulated to last a long time, whereas others are designed to rapidly break down into inert chemicals once they have done their job. Some of these products will kill fleas on contact, whereas others are insect growth regulators (IGRs) that prevent flea eggs from hatching and the larvae from growing into egg-laying adults.

Heartworm prevention medication is available from your veterinarian.

Many scientific advances have been recently made in the development of pesticides and their delivery systems, and with each of these come some advantages and disadvantages. The following list contains some of the most current flea control chemicals commercially manufactured. You can often find a flea control product that contains two or more of these chemicals for the purposes of combining fast-acting pesticides with those that are long lasting.

Pyrethrins: These chemicals are extracted from flowers and have been used for many years. They act on the nervous system of adult fleas, killing them very rapidly, but they have no residual properties by themselves. They have a very low toxicity to humans and animals and can therefore be used relatively safely. Some companies produce a microencapsulated (time release) form that offers longer-lasting results.

Permethrin: This synthetic pyrethrin has become very widely used recently because it is claimed to be effective against both fleas and ticks (particularly those that carry Lyme disease). Permethrin is absorbed into the skin of the dog and is spread through the fat layer. Some dogs are very sensitive to this. Although Permethrin is known to have residual properties, they are not fast acting, so many times it is used in combination with pyrethrins to get the best of both worlds.

Organophosphates: These are usually considered heavy duty insecticides and are usually toxic to both humans and animals. As a result, these are used mainly as a last resort.

Methoprene: This insect hormone interrupts the life cycle of the flea by preventing the larvae from maturing into adults. Because it is a hormone, it is not considered a poison; however, it does prevent fleas from reproducing.

Because of this, several weeks may pass before it takes effect, as it will not kill the egg-laying adults that are initially present, which will continue to survive until they die of more natural causes.

Imidacloprid: This chemical is available in topically (to the skin) applied liquids, which kill on contact. This insecticide will wash off if your dog goes swimming or if it gets a bath. It is not absorbed into the bloodstream and has a long-lasting effect (about one month). It is selectively toxic to insects but is nontoxic to humans or animals.

Fipronil: This insecticide works like Imidacloprid; however, it is not water soluble and will not come off if your dog gets wet. It can be removed with alcohol or with shampoo. Fipronil will attach itself to the oil in your dog's skin and coat. It is therefore important not to bathe the dog for two days before treatment so that sufficient oil is left on its skin and coat to absorb the chemical. It can be safely used on puppies, kittens, dogs, and cats.

Lufenuron: This IGR prevents fleas in their various stages from producing *chitin*. Chitin comprises approximately 30 percent of the flea's body weight and is the major component of the flea's exoskeleton. When Lufenuron is used, flea eggs are unable to hatch because the teeth of the pupae inside the egg are made of chitin, and they are therefore unable to eat their way out of the shell. Likewise, when the larvae molt, they are unable to produce new exoskeletons and thus rapidly perish. This material does not have any adulticidal activity. It is only available through a veterinary prescription, and unlike all of the other chemicals listed in this section, it is administered orally in the pet's food. It comes in tablet form for dogs and a liquid suspension for cats and is effective for one month. The dosage is absorbed in the intestinal tract of the dog and transferred via the bloodstream to the outer tissue layers. If an adult flea bites the treated dog, it ingests the IGR and its progeny will be unable to develop into adults. Because this chemical only affects the eggs and larvae, it will take four to five weeks to break the life cycle and reduce a significant portion of the flea infestation.

Flea-control products come in a wide variety of forms. Likewise, some products are available in retail outlets, whereas others are only available from your veterinarian. Because no flea-control method is 100 percent effective, you will probably find that you will have to combine several approaches to get satisfactory results. You must also keep in mind that there are also regional differences among fleas, and you may want to seek the advice of a local veterinarian or dog groomer to see what product is known to be effective in your area. You may also find that you will have to switch your approach occasionally, because using the same products over and over can lead to a buildup of immunity among the fleas.

Regardless of the method you choose, the first line of defense is regular vacuuming and emptying of the vacuum bags. This step will help eliminate eggs and reduce the food sources for flea larvae. If you detect fleas early enough, you may be able to use powders and sprays directly on your dog and in areas of your house where your dog frequently stays. However, for severe flea problems, it usually takes the following approach to solve the problem:

1. Dip your pet to eliminate the majority of adult fleas on the dog;

2. Simultaneously, have your carpets cleaned to eliminate potential food, and launder all bedding and other washable items which may harbor fleas;

3. Use a residual spray or IGR to prevent a recurrence of the problem; and

4. Consult your veterinarian on the administration of an ingestible IGR, such as Lufenuron.

Lice are also bloodsuckers, and will cause your dog a great deal of irritation. Unlike fleas, however, lice do not jump, but instead tend to burrow into a dog's skin. If a dog becomes infested with lice, you will be able to see clusters of eggs glued onto the dog's hair. The lice will make small wounds that can become infected. Severe infestations of lice can be very dangerous to a Shih Tzu, so bring your dog to a veterinarian promptly if you spot them. Your dog can then be treated with a special insecticidal dip, or dusting, which is designed to eliminate lice.

Ticks are dangerous bloodsucking parasites that can be found in just about all countries worldwide. However, they are much more prevalent in tropical or subtropical climates. When a tick gets onto your dog, it will imbed its head in the dog's skin and hang on tenaciously. In the United States, the most common tick a dog encounters is the brown dog tick. However, in certain areas of the country, there has been an increase in the number of deer ticks found on dogs. Both of these ticks can be carriers of serious diseases that the dog owner should be concerned with.

The brown dog tick is large enough to see with the human eye. This tick has been implicated as a carrier of such diseases as Rocky Mountain spotted fever and babesiasis; however, not all of these ticks carry diseases. Both of these diseases have similar symptoms. In dogs, these diseases will cause fever, anorexia, depression, lethargy, and a rapid pulse rate.

The deer tick is much smaller than the brown dog tick, and it is barely perceptible to the human eye. Deer ticks are not widespread throughout the country, but instead are localized in the northeastern and midwestern regions of the United States. They are a potential health threat in these areas because they may carry Lyme disease. Lyme disease is named after the Connecticut town where the ailment was first noted in humans. The symptoms of this disease are stiffness, pain, fever, rashes, and inflammation of the joints. If diagnosed early enough, Lyme disease can be cured with antibiotic therapy.

Recently, cases of tick-borne diseases have been on the rise. This is most likely due to an increasing number of host animals (mice, raccoons, deer, and opossums, to name a few) moving into areas where they have previously been scarce. Ticks will then breed and leave the animal they have infected, seeking a new host such as a dog or a human.

Humans cannot catch a tick-borne disease from an infected dog. However they could become infected should they be bitten by the same tick that is transmitting the disease. It is impossible to eradicate ticks from all areas, but it is prudent to keep your dog away from known tick-infested areas such as open fields and woods. It is also a good practice to inspect your dog for ticks each time it returns to the house. Be sure to check inside the ears and between the toes, as these areas are preferred by ticks.

To remove a tick, first wash the infected area with alcohol, which helps to loosen the tick's grasp. When you have loosened it somewhat, place a pair of tweezers squarely over the head of the tick, as close to the dog's skin as possible. Carefully lift the tick off the dog, being careful not to pull the body apart. It must be removed in whole condition. If the head remains under the skin, it can cause an infection. Once the tick has been removed, place it in the middle of your toilet and flush. If you suspect the tick of being a carrier of disease, however, you should place it in a tightly sealed jar, and bring it to your veterinarian for examination. Never attempt to remove a tick with a lighted match. Likewise, you should never attempt to remove a tick with your fingers, because it is possible to contract diseases through contact with the tick. If your dog shows signs of tick-borne diseases, take it to the veterinarian immediately.

Mites are very small parasitic creatures that do their damage by burrowing into a dog's skin, causing intense itching. Mites are actually no bigger in size than a pinhead, but when they burrow into the skin in large numbers, they can create a serious skin disease called mange. There are two principal forms of mange that can be found on dogs. One is called sarcoptic, and the other is called demodectic mange.

Sarcoptic mange is usually easier to recognize because it makes a dog more miserable and causes more scratching. The skin in the affected area becomes dry, thickened, wrinkled, and crusty. As the dog scratches, the area will become red and full of bloody sores. The hair will shed completely from the area. As the mites lay eggs in the skin, and as the eggs hatch, the mange will begin to spread. As the spreading continues, the dog will develop an odor similar to that of strong cheese, or that associated with a human foot problem.

Demodectic mange is harder to detect because it may only result in slight hair loss, reddening, and some inflammation of the skin. Sometimes bloody pimples form that can burst and become infected. Demodectic mange may not always cause a great deal of irritation and itching. Even though its symptoms are less noticeable, demodectic mange is usually the harder to cure.

Your veterinarian can identify either form of mange by taking a skin scraping and examining it under a microscope. Once the type of mange is identified, proper treatment can begin.

Other Skin Disorders

When a dog scratches and chews its skin, the cause is not always external parasites. Symptoms such as red dots, pimples, damp spots,

If a problem arises, your veterinarian should be the one to examine your dog's eyes.

crusty and scaly skin, greasy skin, or a loss of hair, may indicate that the dog has eczema.

Eczema is a general name given to several different skin conditions. Eczema occurs in both wet and dry patches, and may have many causes including external parasites. Nutritional deficiencies, hormonal imbalances, excessive heat or dampness, and allergies can all cause these skin conditions. In order to cure an eczema problem, the specific cause must be found and treated.

Another cause of skin problems is called ringworm. Ringworm is actually not a worm at all. It is a fungus that affects the outer layer of skin, hair, and nails. It may cause inflammation, itching, hair loss, and scabby areas. Certain forms of ringworm can be transmitted to humans, so prompt veterinary treatment is essential. Should your dog be diagnosed as having ringworm, it would be advisable to have all humans who come into contact with the dog also diagnosed and treated at once.

Digestive Disorders

Constipation

Constipation occurs when solid waste products build up in a dog's digestive tract and cannot be passed easily. In most cases, constipation can be relieved by changing your Shih Tzu's diet and giving it a mild laxative. Half a

Keep an eye out for symptoms of a possible ear infection.

cup of lukewarm milk every hour is usually very effective. You should also reduce the amount of dry bulk foods in your dog's diet until the stool is normal.

Constipation may also occur if a dog eats an indigestible object, such as a small toy or a stone. If you suspect this, contact your veterinarian immediately. Do not give a laxative if you suspect a foreign object. This may require surgery.

Enteritis

Enteritis is a general term given to any inflammation of the intestinal tract. This inflammation can be caused by bacteria, worms, poisons, ulcers, the swallowing of sharp objects, and so on. Many times enteritis is accompanied by diarrhea or foul-smelling stools. This condition can cause the dog much discomfort, resulting in its lying in unusual and contorted positions when at rest. Almost all intestinal ailments require professional care, so if you notice

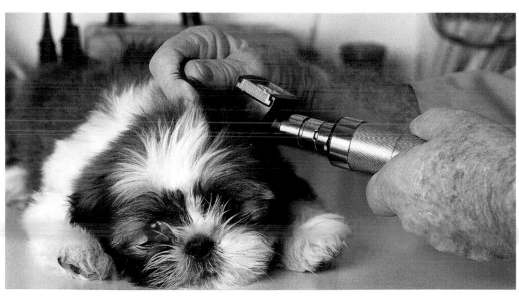

these symptoms, contact your veterinarian immediately.

Respiratory Ailments

Dogs can contract many common throat and respiratory ailments, including coughs, asthma, bronchitis, laryngitis, and pneumonia. They do not, however, suffer from the common cold. Respiratory ailments are characterized by sneezing, coughing, runny nose, watery eyes, slight fever, and chills.

Many of the respiratory ailments that dogs suffer from are the result of other diseases, such as distemper or kennel cough. Most respiratory ailments that plague dogs can be treated with antibiotics. Take your dog to the veterinarian if it shows signs of severe respiratory problems.

Tonsillitis

Tonsillitis (an inflammation of the tonsils) is usually caused by an infection. A dog with tonsillitis may run a high fever, refuse to eat, drool, and vomit frequently and violently. Canine tonsillitis can be treated very effectively using medications, and only rarely is surgery required.

Pneumonia

Once a common killer of dogs, pneumonia can now be successfully treated using antibiotics. This condition is usually caused by a primary virus which attacks the respiratory tract, followed by a secondary bacterial infection. This ailment is usually not considered as pneumonia until after the bacterial invasion has taken place. Symptoms of pneumonia include coughing, shallow breathing, nasal discharge, loss of appetite, and fever.

Ear and Eye Disorders

Ear and eye disorders are extremely uncommon in Shih Tzu. If you do suspect a problem, however, leave your dog's ears and eyes alone and contact your veterinarian. An inexperienced owner who probes too far into the ear canal or accidentally rubs against the eye can cause the dog additional damage.

Eye problems are characterized by watery eyes, discoloration, fluttering eyelids, haziness or opacity of the lens, or a discharge of sticky mucus from the eye. Symptoms of ear disorders include persistent head shaking, cocking the head at an unusual angle, any discharge from the ear, and rubbing of the ears with paws or on the floor. Some ear infections will make the inside of the dog's ears appear reddish and inflamed.

Other Disorders

Umbilical Hernias

One of the few hereditary or genetically carried disorders that plague the Shih Tzu breed is umbilical hernia. These hernias are characterized by the presence of an abnormal opening in the dog's abdomen, which allows part of the abdominal contents to protrude through. This opening is usually the result of a birth defect. The problem can be surgically corrected once the Shih Tzu is six months of age. The procedure consists of stitching the opening closed. If the opening is very small, your veterinarian may elect to put off surgery to see if it closes on its own. If surgery is performed, the Shih Tzu's activities will have to be restricted for a couple of weeks following the operation.

Since this ailment may be hereditary, breeding dogs that have been diagnosed with this disorder should be avoided. It is never a good idea to risk perpetuating a genetic defect in any breed.

False Pregnancy

As the name implies, a false pregnancy is a condition in which a female does not have a fetus in her uterus, but acts as if she were pregnant. She may creep off by herself, become restless, and paw at her bed. The female also tends to carry toys, stuffed animals, or an old shoe into her bed, and defend them as if they were puppies. In extreme cases, she may even begin to lactate.

False pregnancies usually occur about two months after estrus, and may occur after every subsequent estrus cycle. Usually this condition disappears by itself, and a female will return to her normal behavior. If false pregnancies occur several times a year, or if the dog should become overly aggressive in protecting her "offspring," then take her to the veterinarian. While this condition is a result of hormone imbalances, hormone therapy is not recommended for nonbreeder females, as it may cause further complications.

Your veterinarian may suggest the surgical removal of the uterus and ovaries. This is safe, will prevent the reoccurrence of false pregnancy, and may even prolong her life. Numerous false pregnancies can cause your dog a great deal of discomfort, and can lead to uterine infections. The surgery should not be performed while the symptoms of this condition are still apparent, because the protective behavior may persist. Postpone surgery until all symptoms have disappeared.

Shock

Shock is a serious condition that results from a traumatic physical or emotional experience. In medical terms, the word shock is used to describe a state of collapse characterized by a failure of proper blood flow to body tissues. The specific metabolic events that lead to shock are unknown, but it can occur following many forms of serious stress such as burns, heart failure, dehydration, anesthesia, and intestinal obstructions, as well as many others. The most common cause for dogs is automobile accidents. A dog in shock may appear asleep, or it may be semiconscious. The symptoms of shock will vary, depending on the severity of the cause. They include apathy, shallow breathing or rapid respiration, rapid pulse, and the dog's body temperature may drop, making the body feel cold.

If your dog is in shock, try to calm it in a soft, reassuring voice, pet it softly, and keep it warm by covering it with a blanket or an article of clothing. The actions of a dog in shock are often unpredictable, so use caution when handling it. Take it immediately to a veterinarian. Dogs that are treated for shock should be monitored carefully for some time following recovery because serious relapses can occur.

Broken Bones

Broken bones are also a frequent result of automobile accidents. A dog with a fracture will be in severe pain, so be sure to approach the animal with extreme caution, as it may attempt to bite. If a dog has a compound fracture (one in which the broken bone punctures the skin), cover the wound with gauze or a clean cloth to help prevent infection. Broken bones are often accompanied by additional complications, so take your dog immediately

to a veterinarian. Besides setting the broken bones, your veterinarian will perform additional procedures. If there is any bleeding, he or she will attempt to control the hemorrhage, administer antibiotics to prevent infections, and clean and close the wound. If the accident is severe, then surgery may have to be performed to repair the damage. In addition, your veterinarian may have to treat the dog for shock.

Poisoning

Due to the abundance of potentially toxic materials found in our modern society, it would be impossible to cover the causes and symptoms of poisonings in great detail. Instead, this section contains general information on the subject.

If your mature Shih Tzu is suffering from a terminal illness, you may have to make the difficult decision to put an end to its pain.

It is important for you to call directory assistance and obtain the telephone number of the nearest poison control center. Many poisons are fatal if not treated quickly, so keep this number easily accessible in case of emergency. If you suspect that your Shih Tzu has ingested or come into contact with a poison, call the poison control center for the proper antidote. You can then relay this information to the veterinarian. Based on this information, the dog's life may be saved by pumping its stomach, inducing vomiting or diarrhea, or by neutralizing the poison with the appropriate medication.

If you do not know the toxin, call your veterinarian and describe the symptoms. Common symptoms of poisoning are stomach pains, which may cause howling or whimpering, vomiting, diarrhea, convulsions, tremors, and labored breathing.

One of the most common poisons ingested by dogs is rodent poison, which is usually an anticoagulant (meaning that it prevents blood from clotting properly). Symptoms include blood in the urine, stool, and vomit, and nose bleeding. Such poisoning can quickly prove fatal, and a veterinarian can help only if the dog has ingested a very small amount of the poison.

Some pesticides may also be extremely poisonous. Most pesticides will carry a warning on the label as to their potential hazard to humans and animals. Store all pesticides away safely. Keep your dog away from treated plants for at least two weeks after spraying. Pesticide poisonings are characterized by cramps, diarrhea, shortness of breath, and dizziness.

Another common cause of poisoning is antifreeze. While it may seem odd that a dog should come into contact with such a product, dogs are evidently quite attracted to antifreeze. They seem to love the taste. While antifreeze itself is not poisonous, a dog's body converts it into several toxic substances that can cause irreversible kidney damage and eventually death.

There are numerous plants that are poisonous if ingested by your Shih Tzu. These include some laurels, poison hemlock, some milkweeds, deadly nightshades, and dogsbane, as well as several others. Some houseplants may even be potentially harmful. As a general rule, never let your dog eat any questionable plants. If your dog does eat a plant and becomes ill, you may have to get a sample of the plant and have it identified before proper treatment can begin.

Although not poisonous, bee and wasp stings can cause an irritating swelling, trembling, and circulatory failure. If your dog is stung in the throat area, swelling can occur that could lead to suffocation. Bring the dog to the veterinarian immediately.

Nursing a Dog

During the course of your long and loving relationship with your Shih Tzu, it may become necessary for you to act as your dog's nurse when it is sick or recuperating from an illness. In order to competently care for an ill dog, there are several procedures that you should know, including taking the dog's temperature, determining its pulse, and administering medication. However, before you can perform these medical procedures, you must first learn the proper way to handle your dog.

Lay the dog's head in the crook of your arm and hold it firmly. While doing this, make your Shih Tzu feel calm and at ease by speaking softly to it and patting it gently. Use your hand and forearm to hold the dog securely while keeping your other arm completely free to perform additional duties.

When taking your dog's temperature, it must be done rectally, so you may need someone to help you. Taking your dog's temperature will enable you to determine if your Shih Tzu has a fever or hypothermia (subnormal temperature). Hypothermia may be a symptom of poisoning.

The only equipment you will need is a digital rectal thermometer and some petroleum jelly.

When administering a pill to a convalescing Shih Tzu, do not exert too much pressure when prying open the jaws. Place the pill in the back of the dog's mouth, but do not force it into the throat, which could cause the dog to choke.

Once the dog is calm and held securely in place, lubricate the thermometer with the petroleum jelly, lift the dog's tail, and slip the thermometer in. Leave it there for the prescribed length of time before removing it. If your Shih Tzu is acting restless, have someone else try to calm it and hold it as previously described. Then you can lift the tail and remove the thermometer. Wash it in cold water when you are finished.

The normal body temperature of an adult Shih Tzu is between 101.5 and 102.5°F (38.6–39.2°C). The temperature may be slightly higher in younger dogs, and slightly lower in older dogs. A restless dog may have an elevated temperature of a degree or so. Unless the temperature is several points higher than normal, there is usually no need to be alarmed.

When taking your Shih Tzu's pulse, it is best to feel on the inside of the front paw, or the thigh on the same side as the heart. An adult Shih Tzu has a pulse rate of 100 to 120 beats per minute, while younger dogs may have a slightly quicker pulse. In a calm, healthy Shih Tzu, the pulse should feel strong and steady. A weak pulse may indicate poisoning, while an irregular, pounding pulse is a symptom of fever or infection.

The final procedure you should know when nursing a sick dog is how to get the patient to take its medicine. Administering pills or liquid drugs to a dog may be easier said than done. Blessed is the pet owner whose dog voluntarily eats or drinks its medications. Under most circumstances, it takes patience, persistence, and ingenuity to get a finicky Shih Tzu to take its medicine.

Oral medications can come in liquid, tablets, pills, capsules, powders, or paste form. Sometimes a dog will take its medication straight from your hand. If not, you might try mixing it with the dog's food or water (provided your pet has not fallen off its diet). Should these methods fail, you will have to administer it in another way.

Powdered medications can be mixed with water and, like liquid dosages, drawn into a syringe without a needle on it. Open the lips on the side of your Shih Tzu's mouth near its molars. Then, while gently holding the dog's muzzle shut, let the liquid flow slowly into the space between the molars. Allow your dog time to swallow, making sure that all of the medication is taken. *Never* squirt the liquid into the mouth. This can cause coughing or choking, and will make the dog more resistant to taking its next dose of medicine.

If your dog refuses to take pills, tablets, or capsules, try putting them inside a small clump of hamburger or other meat. Never walk away from your dog until you are absolutely sure that the medicine has been swallowed. Some dogs will actually hide the pill inside their mouth and spit it out when you are not looking.

If all else fails, you may have to force your dog to swallow a pill. This must be done in such a way as to prevent the patient from becoming frantic or upset, or else the job will be twice as hard. Hold the dog's upper jaw and, using a minimal amount of pressure, tilt the dog's head backward and upward. This will cause the dog's lower jaw to drop and its mouth will open. Quickly place the pill on the back of the tongue, and hold the mouth closed to prevent the dog from spitting out the pill. Then tilt the head upward and rub, stroke, or massage the dog's throat. This will force the dog to swallow the pill. Do not throw the pill

in because it might accidentally lodge in the windpipe and cause the dog to choke.

Euthanasia

For a dog owner whose pet has been truly loved, the most difficult time is when that devoted friend becomes terminally ill and will soon die. While modern veterinary medicine has numerous ways of extending the life of your pet, you must also be aware that no dog will live forever. In some cases veterinary care may be doing other than extending a dog's life. If your dog should become terminally ill and experience severe and constant pain, most medical attention would not prolong life, but rather would prolong the dying process.

Euthanasia is the act by which a veterinarian can painlessly induce death, ending the suffering of a terminally ill animal. When you must make the painful decision of having your dog put to sleep, consider the animal's feelings as well as your own. This is never an easy choice, and it will probably be made only after deep soul-searching. A caring veterinarian will understand the choices you may have to make, and will be supportive and open for discussion. But remember that the final decision must be yours.

BREEDING YOUR SHIH TZU

Breeding Objectives

The one and only objective of dog breeding is to produce and raise puppies that will uphold the quality of the physical characteristics and temperament of the breed. In simpler terms, your breeding objective should be to create the "perfect" Shih Tzu. In order to do this, you will first have to familiarize yourself with the Shih Tzu Standard.

The Shih Tzu Standard is a complete written description of the breed: how it should look, act, and move. Of course, no one has ever produced the "perfect" Shih Tzu, and most likely, no one ever will. The Standard, however, establishes a goal for which all serious breeders strive. The Shih Tzu Standard, which is used in the United States, was prepared by the American Shih Tzu Club, and approved by the AKC. Every breed recognized by the AKC has its own Standard by which it is judged in competition.

Serious Shih Tzu breeders attempt to improve their dogs through selective breeding with quality dogs from other well-run kennels. Their main goal is to develop a bloodline of their own that is strong in the written breed characteristics of the Standard. The importance of having a written Standard becomes clear if one considers the following scenario. What would happen if 100 breeders were asked to produce what they considered to be the perfect Shih Tzu? As you can imagine, the Shih Tzu would be just about as different as their breeders, and with each subsequent generation, these differences would become greater and greater. Without the Standard, every breed would quickly lose its identity. Adherence to the Standard separates conscientious breeders from unscrupulous ones.

It never seems to fail that in every endeavor of man, there is always someone who will do anything for a quick dollar. Dog breeding is no exception. There are indeed unscrupulous breeders, who are more interested in profits than in the quality and well-being of their puppies. They are not concerned with adhering to the Standard; they are only concerned with creating as many puppies as they can, as quickly as possible. This results in inferior litters that are not of proper physical proportions. Careless breeding will also bring about behavioral abnormalities. In the end, not only do these breeders ruin the reputation of the breed, but they also increase the already heartbreaking number of unwanted dogs.

This female Shih Tzu is surrounded by a litter of adorable puppies.

Characteristics

The following descriptions are based on my interpretation of the AKC-approved Shih Tzu

Standard. My interpretation, however, may not necessarily be the same as a dog-show judge's. If you plan to enter your Shih Tzu in a conformation competition, obtain a copy of the Shih Tzu Standard from the AKC. If you choose to enter your dog in a show competition, remember that only the judge's interpretation of the Standard will decide the winners.

General appearance: The Shih Tzu should be sturdy, live, and alert, with a long, flowing double coat. Due to its noble heritage as the palace pet of several Chinese dynasties, the Shih Tzu has a "distinctively arrogant carriage." The Shih Tzu will move with its head held high and its tail curved over its back. While a certain amount of variation in size is accepted, the Shih Tzu must be "compact, solid, carrying good weight and substance."

The Shih Tzu, even though a toy breed, is to be judged using the same requirements for structure and soundness as prescribed for all breeds. Naturally, any deviations from the ideals of the Standard will be penalized. In addition, any commonly known structural fault will be penalized, regardless of whether such faults are specifically listed in the Standard.

Size, proportion, substance: The Shih Tzu should have a height at the withers (the highest point of the shoulders) of between 8 and 11 inches (20.3–27.9 cm), although ideally it should be between 9 and 10½ inches (22.9–26.7 cm). Mature dogs should weigh between 9 and 16 pounds (4.0–7.26 kg). The length of the Shih Tzu, from the withers to the base of the tail, should be slightly longer than its height at the withers. It should not appear too "leggy," nor should it appear "dumpy or squatty." Regardless of size, the Shih Tzu should always be "compact, solid, and it should carry good weight and substance."

Head: The head of the Shih Tzu should be round, broad, and wide between the eyes. The top of the head must be domed. The head must be in proportion to the rest of the body, and should appear neither too large nor too small. The facial expression will impart a "warm, sweet, wide-eyed, friendly, and trusting" feeling. An overall well-balanced expression will supersede the importance of any individual part. In this section, the judges are warned to look beyond the hair in order to determine the size of the Shih Tzu's head and expression, and not to be deceived by any clever grooming techniques.

Eyes: The eyes must be large, round, placed well apart and looking straight ahead; however, they should not be too prominent. They should be very dark in color; however, on liver- and blue-coated dogs, the eyes may be lighter.

Ears: The proper Shih Tzu ears should be large, heavily coated, and slightly below the crown of the domed skull.

Muzzle: The muzzle must be set no lower than the bottom rim of the eye. It should be square, short, smooth, and with good "cushioning," and must never be downturned. The overall length of the muzzle should be no more than 1 inch (2.5 cm) from the tip of the nose to the stop (the base of the forehead). The length will vary in proportion to the overall size of the dog. The front of the muzzle should be flat. The lower lip and chin should not be protruding, nor should it ever be receding. The jaw is broad and wide, while its bite should be undershot. Missing or slightly misaligned teeth will not be severely penalized. Teeth and tongue should be hidden when mouth is closed.

Nose: The nose, like the lips and eye rims, is black. However, on liver-pigmented dogs, it should be liver-colored, and blue on blue-pigmented dogs. A Shih Tzu's nostrils are broad, wide, and open.

Neck, topline, and body: Once again, the overall balance is of the utmost importance. The neck should be sturdy and flow smoothly into the shoulders. Its length should allow the dog to hold its head high, and should be in proportion to the height and length of the dog. Its back should be level and parallel to the ground. The body is short and sturdy, and there should be no evidence of a waist line or "tuckup." The body should be slightly longer than the tail.

Shih Tzu possess a broad and deep chest with good rib spring. It should not, however, be barrel-chested. The depth of the rib cage should extend to just below the elbow. The distance from the elbows to the withers is slightly longer than from the elbows to the ground. The croup (the highest part of the rump) should be flat.

Tail: The tail is set high on the hindquarters, and heavily "plumed." It should be carried in a curve well over the back.

Forequarters: The shoulders are laid back, well angulated, laid in, and fit smoothly into the body. The forelegs are straight, muscular, and well-boned. Due to the broad chest, they should be set well apart; however, the elbows must be close to the body. The pasterns (the equivalent of a forearm) are strong and perpendicular to the ground. The feet of a Shih Tzu are firm, well padded, and point straight ahead. Dewclaws are allowed to be removed.

Hindquarters: The angle and position of the hindquarters should be in balance with that of the forequarters. The rear legs, like the forelegs, are well-boned and muscular. When viewed from the rear, with the stifles (the equivalent

of the human knee) well bent, the legs should be straight and not close together, but still in line with the forelegs. The hocks (the next joint below the stifle) are "well letdown" and perpendicular to the ground. The rear feet are firm, padded, and pointed straight forward. Dewclaws may be removed.

Coat: A Shih Tzu's double coat is long, luxurious, thick, and flowing. A slight wave is permissible. The hair on top of the head is tied up. Trimming of the hair on the feet, bottom of the coat, and around the anus is allowed for purposes of neatness and to facilitate movement. All coat colors are permissible and should be judged equally.

Gait: This breed should move straight, and must be shown at its natural speed in order to evaluate its "smooth, flowing, and effortless movement." The dog should have a good reach and equally strong rear drive. Its back should remain level during movement, and its head should be carried high. Even when moving, the tail should remain curved over the back.

Temperament: Because the sole purpose of a Shih Tzu is that of a companion and house pet, the Standard dictates that it is essential that its temperament be "outgoing, happy, affectionate, friendly, and trusting towards all."

Deviations

Since there is no such thing as the perfect Shih Tzu, all dogs that are judged against the Standard are considered to have faults. A fault is anything that negatively affects your Shih Tzu's appearance, movement, or temperament. Hostility, nervousness, shyness, and lack of vitality or self-confidence are all undesirable traits in a Shih Tzu.

Physical faults include: too long or too short legs; a narrow head or one that is too large or small; a long muzzle; an overshot or undershot bite; excessive missing teeth; discoloration of eyes, nose, lips, or eye rims; improper slope of the back; head held low; tail not curved; or any other deviation from the Standard measurements. Many of these are difficult to detect in a puppy; however, with age they become more evident.

It is the judge's job to separate the winners from the rest of the dogs. Should your dog not win, do not take out your frustrations on the dog. After all, the dog has no control over its faults. Just remember that whether inside or outside the ring, the only opinion that matters to your Shih Tzu is yours, not the judge's.

Also keep in mind that all of these faults apply only to bench competitions. They will not

The Shih Tzu has a long, flowing double coat.

prevent your Shih Tzu from competing in Obedience trials.

Breeding Your Female

Breeding is not something that you can learn overnight, or that should be done haphazardly. If you are truly interested in breeding quality Shih Tzu, and are not discouraged by the amount of responsibility you will have to undertake, then contact an experienced breeder. A professional can either help you breed your dog, or teach you some of the finer points of breeding. Under no circumstances should an amateur deliberately breed a female Shih Tzu without the guidance of an experienced breeder. Once you have attained a thorough knowledge of the principles of breeding, contact your local Shih Tzu Club. They can help you find a suitable stud dog, and can be a source of additional valuable information.

The following sections are merely a summary and not an all-inclusive guide to breeding.

Choosing a Mate

Obtain a list of available stud dogs from your Shih Tzu Club, and make appointments to visit as many of these breeders as possible. As you inspect the dogs, study each one for its conformation to the breed Standard. Emphasis should be placed on the overall quality of the dog's heritage.

Prior to visiting the stud dogs, you may want to reexamine your female's conformation, and make notes on her weaknesses when compared to the Shih Tzu Standard. When selecting a stud dog, you should avoid any that have faults similar to those of your female.

Once you have made your choice of a stud dog, you will have to make an agreement with the breeder on a stud fee. Naturally you can expect to pay more for the services of a champion stud dog, and less for a pet-quality animal. Many times, the breeder will demand the pick of the litter as payment rather than money. Either way, the terms of the arrangement should be agreed upon in advance.

When Is Your Female Ready?

You should not breed your female until she is in her second or third season. However, it is important that she be mature enough both

It is up to you to find the right home for every puppy.

physically and mentally to deal with the demands of raising a litter. You should avoid breeding a female Shih Tzu that is significantly less than 18 months old. Likewise, she should not be bred once she is six years old. If you wish to breed her several times when she is young, it should not be more frequently than once a year.

Prior to her estrus, bring your Shih Tzu to the veterinarian to be checked for worms and for any booster shots that she may need. Keep her in top condition and watch her weight carefully. As her season approaches, check her daily for the swelling of her vulva and the appearance of colored discharge. The best time to breed a female is from 9 to 14 days after the first signs of color. In most cases, the highest chance of conception occurs on the twelfth day. The female is ready for mating when the color changes from dark red to yellow.

When the swelling first appears, make an appointment with the owner of the chosen stud dog. Once mating has taken place, do not attempt to separate the dogs if they are still coupled, for injuries can occur. Once the dogs have separated, remove the female and put her in her cage or in

your car. Do not let her urinate for about half an hour after breeding. If the female still appears receptive, she may be bred again a day or two later.

Remember that although your female has been bred, she will continue to have some discharge and will continue to attract other male dogs. Even though she can rarely be bred at this time, it is best to guard her carefully until she is definitely out of season.

The Birth of Puppies

The gestation period of a female Shih Tzu is 58 to 63 days, so you can expect puppies about 9 weeks from the day of mating.

By the fifth or sixth week, you should be able to tell if the mating was successful or not. The abdomen of the pregnant female will begin to swell, and her breasts will become firmer. At this point, you can switch her over to a special whelping diet—as recommended by your veterinarian. After about seven weeks you can begin to cut down on her exercise, but do not eliminate it entirely. Walking can be very beneficial, and mild exercise will maintain her muscle tone.

During the final weeks of her pregnancy, your Shih Tzu should begin to lose the hair around her breasts. This is perfectly normal, and will enable her newborn puppies to find her teats more easily so they can feed. As the big day gets closer, the female's breasts will swell with milk, and the nipples will become darker in color.

When the big event is only a few weeks away, you should introduce the female to her whelping box. Allow her to become accustomed to it during the day and sleep in it overnight. Use the same rules for the materials as you would a sleeping box (see page 14). Line the box with a thick layer of newspapers covered by a clean blanket and some cloth that can be easily changed. Place the box in a warm, quiet, draft-free location. The temperature around the box will have to be maintained at between 70 and 80°F (21–27°C) for at least five weeks after the puppies are born.

In most cases, the mother will let you know when whelping time is near. When this happens, keep her with you or put her in the whelping box and stay with her. Remove all distractions around the box. Eventually she will settle into her box and begin her labor, which includes heavy panting and visible contractions. Soon the first puppy will appear at the vulva, and will slide out with the contraction.

The mother will actually take care of the entire birth process. When the puppy emerges it will be covered with a membrane (amniotic sac). The afterbirth should follow each birth, as it is attached to the puppy by the umbilical cord. Once the first puppy is completely out, the mother will immediately tear open the amniotic sac and shred the umbilical cord with her teeth. She should start licking the puppy as soon as it is free of the sac. This action serves to dry, clean, and stimulate the puppy into breathing. If the mother attempts to eat the afterbirth, allow her to, for this is perfectly natural.

The puppies should be born at regular intervals of about 30 minutes, but deliveries can be as short as 5 minutes, and as long as 2 hours. The average Shih Tzu litter is five to six puppies, but on rare occasions, she may give birth to as many as twelve.

The entire birth process will usually occur without any problems, but on rare occasions, your assistance may be required. Once the newborn has fully emerged, firmly pinch the umbilical cord in the middle using your fingers or a pair of pliers. Next, cut the cord about 2 inches (5 cm) from the puppy's belly, using a pair of scissors. Apply iodine to the end of the cut to prevent infections. Then open the amniotic sac, starting near the puppy's nose, and removing all of the membrane from around the head and body. Gently open the puppy's mouth and carefully remove any mucus that may be obstructing the breathing passages. Finally, wrap the puppy in a warm towel and rub briskly, concentrating on the ribs and chest, for about 15 minutes, to stimulate breathing. Be sure not to exert too much pressure when rubbing.

Puppy Care

When Shih Tzu puppies are born, they cannot see or hear. Your puppies will remain sightless for about ten days, and although they can crawl, it will be more than a week before they are able to stand. It will take a full four weeks before your puppies gain full control of their senses.

Up until this time the puppies will be totally dependent on their mother. She will nurse them, clean them, and even lick up their excretion in order to keep the whelping box clean. You are only needed to change the box linings as soon as they become soiled.

During their fourth week your puppies will become more aware of their environment, and naturally they will be very curious about it. They can see and hear now, and have better control of their motor functions.

You can now start to wean them. Weaning means that the puppies stop depending on their mother for food and begin to eat on their own. Begin the weaning process as soon as possible because it will not be long before the mother's milk supply runs short.

The easiest method is to purchase a high-quality commercial puppy food, and soften it with hot water. Mix it until it is of a thin consistency and lukewarm in temperature. Place the mixture in a large, flat dish, and put the puppies around it. Dip your finger into the mixture and smear some on the end of each puppy's nose. It doesn't take long before the puppies get the message. They will begin to sniff at the plate, and finally eat from it.

Once the puppies are eating on their own, you should start to cut back on the amount of water you add to the food. Gradually decrease the water until the puppies are eating dry food. Once they have reached this stage, you can begin to add fresh meats or canned puppy food to their diet.

When the puppies start to feed themselves, they will begin to lose the passive immunity that they were receiving from their mother's milk. So by the time they are six or seven weeks old, they will have to make their first trip to the veterinarian for a series of temporary shots. Also bring a few stool samples so the veterinarian can check for worms. If worming is needed, your veterinarian will direct you on how to medicate your puppies.

Once the puppies are seven weeks old, they will have to leave the comfort and safety of their mother and littermates, and find new homes. Your Shih Tzu Club may be able to supply you with a list of potential buyers, or they can help you find good homes for the pups.

UNDERSTANDING YOUR SHIH TZU

Early History

The exact origins of the Shih Tzu are really unknown. However, there is enough evidence available to create a theory that most experts feel is accurate. There are documents, paintings, and other art objects of Chinese origin that contain references to and images of a form of dog believed to be the original ancestor of the modern Shih Tzu. The oldest documents date back to the Tang Dynasty, in the year 624 A.D. It indicates that a pair of these dogs was given to the royal court by a Chinese nobleman. It is believed that the nobleman obtained the dogs from the ancient empire of Byzantium. Unfortunately there is little further documentation for well over three centuries thereafter. The next mention of these dogs (or a breed that was very similar) comes in the years 990–994 A.D., when the people of the Ho Chou province gave them to the Imperial Court as a tribute. It is believed that the dogs were bred in the forbidden city of Peking for several centuries.

There are later records written during the Manchu Dynasty of the mid-seventeenth century. They claim that early relatives of the Lhasa Apso were brought from Tibet to the forbidden

The Shih Tzu's history is linked to characteristics of its present-day behavior.

city. The highly prized Apsos were given as gifts by the Dalai Lama of Tibet, as well as taken by Manchu generals as spoils of war. Such dogs were placed at the feet of the emperor as a sign of fealty, or as a symbol of conquest. It is believed that these Tibetan Apsos were bred with the native dogs of the Chinese royal palace.

It is possible that during these years of breeding by the royal family, several other crossbreeds may have occurred. The original ancestors may have been a relative of the Chinese Pekingese, or at least, at one point in time, there were some crosses with this breed. It is also believed that in the Imperial Palace there were some crosses with a smooth coated breed that was the ancestor of the modern Pug. Whether these crosses were intentional or not, they definitely played an important part in the origins of our modern Shih Tzu.

There are several pictures of a small, lion-faced dog that appear in the Imperial Dog Book of the Manchu Dynasty, and there are records indicating that these special dogs were selected with great care for court breeding. From these came the Shih Tzu that we know today. While the word Shih Tzu is Chinese for lion dog, they were often referred to as the chrysanthemum-faced dog. One look at a Shih Tzu groomed in the traditional Chinese manner will tell you why.

This method consists of combing out the dog's mustache and beard away from the face, and roughing up the hair behind the head and on the shoulders to form a large, puffed-up head of fur that resembles the aforementioned flower.

The writings in the Imperial Dog Book tell of how these small, intelligent, and docile dogs were bred by court eunuchs. They would compete with each other to produce specimens for the Emperor. If a dog caught the Emperor's eye, a picture of it would be placed in the court record book. This was considered a very great honor, indeed.

It is known that the Shih Tzu was a highly favored house pet of the royal family for well over two centuries. However, during the Revolution, many dogs were destroyed because they were viewed as a symbol of imperial rule. Only a few of the royal dogs escaped.

In 1930, Lady Brownrigg, an Englishwoman living in China, was able to save a pair of Shih Tzu and import them to England. Their names were Hibou (the male) and Shu-Ssa. Shortly afterward, another male, named Lung-Fu-Ssu, was imported into Ireland. Later in the 1930s, a few more Shih Tzu were saved by an English officer on duty in China. All of the Shih Tzu we know of today are descendants of these dogs. In 1934, the Shih Tzu Club of England was formed, and the first championship awards were given in 1940.

From England, the breed spread to Scandinavia, to other European countries, and to Australia. During World War II, members of the armed forces stationed in England were introduced to the breed, and they brought a few back to the United States. It was not until 1950 that a considerable number of Shih Tzu were imported into the United States. Not only did they come from England, but a large number also came from France, Denmark, and Sweden.

The Shih Tzu was recognized as a separate breed by the American Kennel Club in 1955. Once recognized, they were allowed to be shown in the Miscellaneous Class, which no longer exists. In 1957, the Shih Tzu Club of America was formed. The Shih Tzu was admitted registration to the AKC Stud Book in March, 1969, and obtained its regular show classification in the Toy Group in September, 1969.

As you can see, the Shih Tzu has only a short history outside of China. Shih Tzu were not known to the western world prior to 1930, because it was literally impossible to obtain one during the reign of the Chinese emperors. These dogs were the personal property of the royal family, and anyone who attempted to acquire one illegally was usually put to death. Since 1930, however, this favorite breed of the royal Chinese courts has quickly spread in popularity.

In 1952, an intentional crossbreeding of the Shih Tzu with a Pekingese took place in England. This was done because there were so few Shih Tzu in Great Britain that some breeders felt there was a danger of the dogs becoming seriously inbred. Many Shih Tzu at this time were suffering from poor bone structure, poor pigmentation, and pinched nostrils. It was felt that a cross with a Pekingese would help improve these problems and, at the same time, would not alter any of the other traits that characterize the breed.

In 1957, the English Kennel Club introduced a rule that allowed all Shih Tzu that were four generations removed from the Pekingese cross to compete as pure Shih Tzu. The American Kennel Club, however, was not nearly as lenient. They would not recognize any dog that did not have a ten-generation purebred Shih Tzu pedigree. In any event, there have been no further crosses, and all of the purebred Shih Tzu of today have greater than ten generations between themselves and the Pekingese cross.

Instinctive Behavior

All dogs, regardless of breed, can trace their ancestry back to a form of wild dog or wolf. As previously mentioned, these creatures lived in a specially structured society. To live together in harmony, the members of each pack had to conform to certain behavioral rituals. These rituals included ranking order and the marking of territories. After the passing of countless generations of these wild dogs, these behavioral patterns eventually became instinctive. It is because dogs possess these instinctive behaviors that man was first able to domesticate them.

Evidence indicates that dogs were first domesticated about 12,000 years ago. Undoubtedly, they were the first of all animals to be tamed by humans. It is believed that humans trained wolves, or wild dogs, to assist them in hunting. The hunting practices of both dogs and humans at this time were probably very similar. This made training them all the more simple.

During the course of domestication, dogs lost many of the behavioral rituals associated with pack life, but retained others. They also began to display new behavior patterns that they learned from their human trainers. Which traits were gained and which were lost depended greatly on the history of each particular breed and its relationship with humans.

Much of the Shih Tzu's history revolved around its association with the imperial family in the forbidden city of Peking. This close relationship with royalty is no doubt responsible for the proud and arrogant manner in which the Shih Tzu moves and behaves. These regal house pets were cherished and pampered by the royal family and their servants for hundreds of years. As a result of countless generations of pampering, the Shih Tzu has also developed a friendly disposition toward all people, a trait not found in all breeds of dogs.

Most of the physical attributes of the Shih Tzu are a result of the careful and select breeding practices used by the eunuchs of the royal court. These breeders would mate dogs based on their temperament as well as their physical qualities. The last thing the royal breeders wanted was to have their prized pooches snap at the emperor.

The nature of the Shih Tzu is, therefore, a blend of two elements. First is the instinctive behavior that has been retained from its wild ancestors. This behavior includes the sexual drive, the marking of territory, and submitting to a ranking order. Second are the traits for which the dog has been selectively bred, such as people-oriented behavior, which is the result of their being bred to become the perfect house pet of the Imperial Courts.

Communication

Dogs are not blessed with the ability to speak an intelligible language, so they must find other ways of communicating their thoughts and emotions to both humans and other dogs. All dogs will use body language, facial expression, and vocal sounds to convey their feelings. In order to understand your dog's moods, you should pay special attention to these signals.

The Shih Tzu's nature is partially a result of instinctive traits inherited from its wild ancestors.

Dogs do not make sounds simply to hear the sound of their own voices. Each noise they make is for a reason. Every sound reflects a mood. A dog will whimper and whine when it is lonely; yelp in fright; howl in pain; groan in contentment; bark in anger, alarm, or glee; and make a variety of sounds when it is seeking attention.

The bark of the Shih Tzu is very unique. Unlike other toy breeds, the Shih Tzu does not exhibit noisy yapping. Instead, it will give one short, sharp bark, which fades into a series of throaty groans. The Shih Tzu will use this sound

As your loving pet ages, it will require your patience and understanding.

to express a variety of moods. Often you must look for additional signs to determine the purpose of the sound.

Body language is another good indicator of your dog's mood. A happy dog may jump up and down and bark. A dog that crouches and lowers its head to the floor may be showing signs of fear. Many times you can get insight into your dog's emotions by examining its tail. A briskly wagging tail is a sign of joy. The happier the dog is, the more its tail will wag. A frightened dog will lower its tail, and perhaps put it between its legs.

As a final indicator of your dog's mood, examine its ears and muzzle. A contented Shih Tzu will have a closed mouth and normally set ears. An alert or attentive dog will raise its ears. Sometimes it will cock its head inquisitively to one side. Should you encounter a dog whose ears are back and upper lips raised exposing the teeth, be very cautious. These are signs of a very frightened or angry dog. Many times these signals precede an attack.

Watch your dog's facial expressions for signs of communication.

The Sense Organs

Most dogs do not have a very good sense of sight. Instead they rely more on their senses of smell, hearing, taste, and touch. Due to its long history as a house dog, the Shih Tzu also lacks much of the ability to discriminate between scents, a sense that is exceptional in some of the larger breeds. The sense of smell is very important to some dogs, such as the hunting or herding dogs. It is, however, of little practical use to a lap dog. Much of the Shih Tzu's ability to discriminate between different scents has simply disappeared due to a lack of use.

What the Shih Tzu lacks in its ability to smell is more than made up for in its ability to hear. The Shih Tzu possesses a highly developed sense of hearing, which is significantly superior to that of a human. They can hear a wider range of sounds, especially those in the high-pitched frequencies. Shih Tzu have no trouble hearing the silent call of the Galton whistle. They can also hear sounds from a much greater distance than a human.

The Shih Tzu does not have the ability to focus its eyes sharply on an object, but its peripheral vision is much greater than that of a human. Because of this, the Shih Tzu's eyes are much more sensitive to motion. They must, however, rely more on their sense of hearing to interpret what they see.

The long coat of the Shih Tzu does not take away greatly from its sense of feeling. These tiny dogs are much more sensitive to touch than many other long-haired breeds. The Shih Tzu's sense of feeling, however, is not as great as that of a human.

It is believed that the Shih Tzu, like all other dogs, may possess other senses that we do not completely understand. One of these is a dog's innate sense of navigation. We have all heard reports of dogs traveling hundreds of miles to find their home, yet we do not fully comprehend how it is done.

Life Changes

In its first weeks in your home, your puppy is extremely impressionable. It is during this time that it begins to learn the rules of the house and starts to form its relationship with its owner. During this time, you will use training as a method of curbing and satisfying your puppy's ever-growing curiosity.

As the puppy continues to grow, it will become more and more aware of its own physical attributes. With the passing of time, your puppy will begin to build up strength and improve its motor skills. Accompanying your dog's improvement in muscle conditioning is an increasing confidence in itself.

By the time your Shih Tzu is 12 or 13 weeks old, it will have become completely aware of itself and its environment. One of its favorite pastimes will be to share all of its discoveries with you. It will begin to investigate everything. During this stage, your puppy is still extremely impressionable, so treat it with care and continue to reinforce the rules of your house. This will be extremely important because of what lies ahead.

At seven to ten months old, your Shih Tzu will almost have reached full size. This is when the dog reaches sexual maturity, a period in time that is the equivalent of human adolescence. No longer will your puppy act with innocent curiosity. Instead, its actions will be bolder and more assertive. Just as a human

Dog/Human Age Equivalents

Dog's Age	Human's Age	Dog's Age	Human's Age
2 months	14 months	7 years	49 years
3 months	3 years	8 years	56 years
6 months	5 years	9 years	63 years
8 months	9 years	10 years	65 years
12 months	14 years	11 years	71 years
18 months	20 years	12 years	75 years
2 years	24 years	13 years	80 years
3 years	30 years	14 years	84 years
4 years	36 years	15 years	87 years
5 years	40 years	16 years	89 years
6 years	42 years	17 years	95 years

teenager might do, your Shih Tzu will begin to test the system. This is when you will start to see just how effective all of your previous training methods have been.

Your Shih Tzu is now feeling extremely comfortable and confident with your lifestyle, and will naturally want to be included in all of your activities. While you have continued to train your puppy, and it should therefore know what is expected of it, there is a growing feeling in your dog that tells it otherwise. It is at this point that your Shih Tzu's instincts tell it that it is time to challenge you in order to improve its rank. Remember, this is all part of the natural ways of canine behavior. When it does occur, do not lose your temper. You must calmly, yet firmly, show your Shih Tzu that you are the authority. This will help lead your dog through its final stage of development.

Once your Shih Tzu reaches full maturity, it should not undergo any behavioral changes (with the exception of mating urges) until a ripe old age. Changes that occur during the geriatric years are more dependent on the individual dog and its medical background. With many aged dogs, changes in their routines or behavior are often the result of a medical problem brought on by old age. As the dog ages, it may undergo a deterioration of the digestive and immune systems, as well as a deteriorating skeletal-muscle condition.

The older dog may become lethargic or moody, lose its orientation, or experience hearing loss. It may even forget many learned responses. This may all sound dreadful, yet it is all part of the aging process. There is very little you can do to change the situation, except offer your devoted, loving pet your sympathy and understanding.

BASIC AND ADVANCED TRAINING

In all honesty, the Shih Tzu may not be as easy to train as some other breeds. However, they are a very intelligent dog, and there is no reason why they cannot learn any lesson you wish to teach them. This chapter will describe some basic rules you must follow, and certain techniques you can use when teaching your Shih Tzu the basic commands and some advanced tricks. This chapter does not cover all of the skills a Shih Tzu can learn, but the same rules and techniques can be implemented to teach your dog an endless number of skills. How much, and how well your Shih Tzu learns will be totally dependent upon your abilities as a trainer.

Why Dogs Learn

Your Shih Tzu has a history and instinctive behavior that goes back into time before they were first domesticated. These wild dogs were pack animals, and as such had to learn to function as a group in order to survive. Their coexistence was dependent upon the establishment of a ranking order that prevented serious fights within the pack. Ranking order is based primarily on strength and experience. In this

Once you find the right training technique, your Shih Tzu should prove to be an eager and intelligent student.

system, smaller and weaker dogs have to submit to dogs of higher authority. Ranking order is an instinctive behavior that is still exhibited in our modern-day domesticated breeds.

During the training process, you will be showing your Shih Tzu that you and other members of your family are the authority to which it must submit. Once your puppy recognizes you as the pack leader, you can teach it the rules of your house.

Training a Puppy

The first lesson, teaching your puppy its name, will begin as soon as you bring the puppy home from the breeder. This will probably be the easiest of all lessons for your dog to understand. Every time you call your puppy, or give it commands, address it by its given name. Try not to call your Shih Tzu by any nicknames. This will only confuse it, and it may not respond when called.

Another early lesson your Shih Tzu will have to learn is the meaning of the word *"No."* It is inevitable that you will have to use this word several times on the first day alone. A mischievous puppy will always do something wrong during its explorations of your home. When this happens, tell it *"No"* in a sharp, firm tone that shows your puppy you are serious. Do not allow the puppy to misinterpret your warnings.

CHECKLIST

The 10 Commandments of Training

In developing your training methods, there are certain do's and don'ts that must be followed. Adhere to these rules during training sessions.

1 **Thou shall maintain a positive atmosphere.** Hold each training session in an atmosphere conducive to learning, with as few distractions as possible. Never attempt to teach your puppy anything when you are in a bad mood.

2 **Thou shall be authoritative.** Your dog will understand tones better than words, and you must deliver all visual and verbal commands clearly and unmistakably. Reprimands must be sharp and firm, whereas praise must be calm and friendly. Never demonstrate your authority by using physical force.

3 **Thou shall be consistent.** All household members must decide what is permitted behavior and what is not. Once your dog has learned a lesson, never let it do the contrary without a reprimand.

4 **Thou shall teach only one new lesson per session.** Do not attempt to teach your puppy more than one new lesson in a single session, and never move onto a new concept until the dog has mastered the previous one. Once a lesson has been mastered, it can be included as a warm-up exercise in your dog's training regimen.

5 **Thou shall give credit where credit is due.** Praise your dog when it performs a command properly. Verbal praise, petting, or scratching behind the ears will make your Shih Tzu an eager student.

6 **Thou shall not stoop to bribery.** Although many trainers coerce their pupils with food, this practice is unnecessary. Enthusiastic praise should be enough incentive.

7 **Thou shall punish disobedience immediately.** Because a puppy has a very short memory, you must never put off a reprimand. If, for example, your puppy chews a slipper, do not punish it unless you catch it in the act; otherwise it will not understand why you are displeased.

8 **Thou shall not hit.** Limit yourself to verbal reprimands; never hit or use physical force on your dog.

9 **Thou shall not bore your students.** Even when your dog is older, keep your training sessions short and end them early if the dog begins to lose interest. Likewise, never hold a training session when your dog is tired.

10 **Thou shall not delay training.** Begin working with your puppy the day you bring it home. Hold two or three sessions each day and hold them for as long as the puppy shows interest. In 10 to 15 minutes, you can provide sufficient teaching without boring the dog.

If the puppy refuses to listen, place it in its cage. *Never* hit your puppy, either with your hand or with a rolled-up newspaper. This will make your puppy fearful of you and hand-shy of anyone who comes near it. Using a cage will simplify training and speed up the housebreaking process.

Walking on a Leash

Because you will be taking your Shih Tzu for its scheduled outdoor elimination sessions, you must teach it how to walk on a leash. Begin this training from the first time you walk the puppy. Place a collar on the puppy, making sure that it is neither too tight nor too loose. Attach the leash, and begin your walk. Hold the leash on your right side and use gentle tugs or pulls to keep the puppy close to your leg. Do not allow the puppy to get under your feet. Also, do not let the puppy run ahead of you. If it tries to run ahead, restrain the puppy by using friendly persuasion with the leash. For the most part, though, your puppy will tend to fall behind because its legs are short and it is not capable of great speed. If your puppy should trail behind, remain patient. Use encouraging words and some gentle force to keep the puppy in the proper walking position.

Being Alone

A puppy must learn at an early age that it will be left alone on occasion. You must teach it how to behave when it is on its own, because a poorly trained puppy can cause a great deal of damage.

To accustom your puppy to being alone, leave it in a familiar room while you quietly go into an adjacent room where the puppy can neither see nor hear you. Stay there for five or ten minutes and then return. If the puppy has gotten into any trouble, reprimand it. Gradually increase the time the puppy is left alone in the room, reprimanding it when necessary, until it begins to act properly.

If you must leave before your puppy has gained your full trust, then place it in its cage with some food, water, and toys until you return. If you do not have a cage, lock the puppy in a familiar puppy-proof room with the same supplies and its sleeping box. Remove all tempting objects such as shoes, papers, and clothing.

No Begging Allowed

It never fails to amaze me just how many people intentionally (or unintentionally) teach their dogs to beg. Some people even think that seeing a dog beg is a cute or innocent act. Begging, however, is neither cute nor innocent. It is a very bad habit that should not be tolerated. A well fed and properly trained dog should never have to beg.

Begging may start out very innocently. You are about to sit down to eat your big, juicy steak when you notice your beloved Fifi standing in the doorway staring at you (and your steak) with watery, pleading eyes. You must resist the temptation! Most people succumb, making a big mistake. They will call their beloved Shih Tzu to the table and reward it with a table scrap. You would not believe how this simple act of charity on your part can turn into such a nasty habit. While you may not mind having Fifi as a constant table companion, think about how it may bother dinner guests in your home.

Begging must be stopped before it develops into a bad habit. If your Shih Tzu attempts to beg for table scraps, reprimand it with a scolding of *"No!"* Then point away from the table and toward the puppy's cage or sleeping box. After a short while, your puppy will learn to avoid the table during mealtimes.

Simple Commands

The simple commands that every puppy must learn are *sit, stay, come, heel,* and *lie down.* You should begin to teach your Shih Tzu these lessons when it is six months old. Hold your

training sessions in a confined area so as to avoid distractions. Try to keep the sessions short (10 to 15 minutes) and limit them to two or three times a day, so you will not wear your puppy out. A tired puppy will be more resistant to learning. Another good tip is to train your puppy before it has eaten. A puppy may become sluggish and disinterested after a big

Your puppy must learn to be left on its own sometimes.

meal. It is also wise to take your puppy for a walk and allow it to eliminate before each session. Learning its lessons will be hard enough without additional pressures.

When teaching your Shih Tzu the simple commands, use one- or two-word phrases when giving orders rather than long sentences. For example, say *"Sit, Fifi"* rather than *"Sit down next to me, Fifi."* Besides keeping the commands short, you must also use the proper tone of voice and gestures. Commands should be clear, firm, and sharp. If you accompany the verbal orders with an easily understood hand gesture, you can eliminate much of the confusion that a puppy might be experiencing.

Sit: The *sit* command can be taught just as easily indoors as outdoors. Fit your puppy with its leash and collar, and take it to an isolated room or a quiet area in your yard. Hold the

When your dog has mastered the come command, it should run to you whenever you give the command.

leash about halfway down in your right hand, and place your left hand on the puppy's hindquarters. Then give the firm, sharp command of *"Sit!"* or *"Sit, Fifi,"* while pressing gently and steadily on its hindquarters. If your puppy begins to lower its head, gently pull the leash upward to prevent it from lying down. Once your puppy is seated, hold it down for a while and do not allow it to jump back up. Be sure to praise your dog thoroughly.

Repeat this procedure for the entire session or until the puppy begins to lose interest. Each time the command is performed, praise your dog's efforts. As your puppy begins to sit without any pressure being applied to its

When teaching your Shih Tzu to sit, press down gently on the hindquarters with one hand while the other hand holds the head upright with the aid of a leash.

hindquarters, you can start to accompany the verbal command with a hand gesture, such as a finger pointed toward the ground.

Do not expect your Shih Tzu to master this lesson in its first training session. If you repeat the procedure every day, your puppy will soon learn to sit. Once you feel confident of your Shih Tzu's abilities, remove the leash and give the command. If your dog has been trained properly, it should perform correctly. If not, remain patient, and repeat the procedure using the leash.

Stay: The *stay* command is usually a more difficult command to learn, especially for a devoted puppy that always wants to be by its owner's side. The *stay* command is very important because, on occasion, a dog's life may depend on obeying it. This command means that the dog should stand stationary wherever it is, and has been used to prevent many dogs from running in front of moving automobiles.

Once again, fit your puppy with its collar and leash. When teaching your puppy to stay, refrain from using its name with the command. On hearing its name, the dog may think that some action is expected from it. Begin this lesson by running through the *sit* procedure. Once the dog is seated, follow this with the command *"Stay!"* As you say this new command, raise your hand, palm toward the dog, like a policeman stopping traffic. Normally your dog will just cock its head and give you a bewildered stare. If the puppy should begin to stand up, however, reproach it with a sharp *"No!"*

Take up all the slack in the leash and hold your Shih Tzu in place. Repeat the procedure until your dog appears to understand. Then remove the leash and repeat the command several times. Each time the dog obeys, praise it. Should it disobey, scold it with a sharp *"No!"*

Continue this procedure until your puppy has repeated it with regular success. Then slowly back away from the dog. As you walk backward, be sure to maintain eye contact with your student, and keep repeating the verbal command *"Stay!"* with your palm raised. Should your Shih Tzu begin to follow, give it a sharp *"Stay!"* If it continues, reprimand it. Naturally, you should give your beloved puppy great praise when it obeys.

Come: If you call out your puppy's name, it will probably race across the room to greet you. The real trick to the *come* command, however, is to have your puppy run to you when something of greater interest is attracting its attention. Your job will be to train your Shih Tzu to come to your side whether it wants to or not.

Teach your Shih Tzu to come right after it has learned to sit and stay. Begin your session by running through the *sit* and *stay* procedures. Once it has stayed at a good distance, call the dog by name followed with the command *"Come."* Accompany the words with a lively sound or gesture such as clapping your hands or bending down and slapping your thighs. This will help excite your dog into motion.

Under most circumstances, your Shih Tzu will quickly learn this lesson, and you should praise each success. If the puppy remains stubborn and does not respond correctly, put it on a long rope and let it wander away. Then repeat the command *"Come,"* and begin to reel the rope in. Continue to repeat the command as the dog is drawn closer. When your puppy reaches your side, shower it with praise. Repeat this lesson several times, and then try it again without the rope.

Obedience Training

Two of the simple commands—*heel* and *down*—are considered part of a dog's obedience training because they are mandatory exercises for every dog that enters an Obedience trial. Even if you do not plan to enter your Shih Tzu in an Obedience trial, there are many obedience exercises that all dogs should learn. These skills will help you to handle your dog properly

Accompany the stay command with the proper hand signal. Be sure to hold your hand at a level that can be easily seen by your student.

in awkward situations, and will reinforce your dog's understanding of the master/subordinate relationship.

Obedience Schools

Do not be misled: Obedience schools are not just for the problem or stubborn dog. These schools can teach both you and your dog all there is to know about competing in shows. Even if you are not planning to enter your Shih Tzu in an Obedience trial, these schools can offer an enjoyable and interesting alternative to training your dog alone. They provide a learning atmosphere and are run by experienced dog handlers who can supply you with expert advice and helpful training tips.

If there is an older child in your family, you can have him or her take your Shih Tzu to classes. This will help teach your child the responsibilities of dog care. Working with a dog at obedience school will teach your child greater self-respect and also respect for the dog.

You can get the name of a reputable obedience school in your area from your Shih Tzu Club or the AKC. Before enrolling, be sure that the class is affordable and suits your purposes. Most schools offer separate classes for owners interested in showing, and others for amateurs.

Heel

When your Shih Tzu learns to heel properly, it will walk on your left side with its head about as far forward as your knees. Heeling prevents your dog from running across your feet and entangling you in the leash, or moving away and bumping into people. Although you will require a leash when you begin to teach this lesson, eventually your Shih Tzu must learn to heel without the restraint of a leash.

Begin by running through all the other commands your dog has mastered. This will help bolster the dog's confidence before you start this difficult lesson. Hold the end of the leash in your right hand, and stand with the dog by your left leg. Then remove all slack from the leash by grabbing the leash about halfway toward the collar with your left hand. Begin to walk briskly (by your Shih Tzu's standards), giving the sharp command *"Heel!"* or *"Heel, Fifi!"* Control and guide the dog's movements using your left hand. Do not allow the dog to run ahead, drop back, or stray from side to side. You must remain patient. Your dog may act unpredictably when faced with this new command.

As the lessons progress, remember to praise your dog for responding correctly, and reprimand it immediately for improper actions. Should your Shih Tzu continue to lag behind, pull steadily on the leash to bring the dog even with your leg. Do not force your dog forward or drag it behind you. This will destroy your dog's confidence. If it lunges forward, pull it back to your side while repeating the *"Heel"* command. If you continue to have difficulty, run through the *sit, stay,* and *come* exercises before trying the *"Heel"* command again.

The *heel* lesson is very difficult for a dog to learn, so remain patient and try not to teach the lesson too quickly. Take your time and be sure your dog understands it thoroughly. Once your Shih Tzu has mastered the *heel* on a leash, take it through a turning exercise. If it has trouble heeling whenever you turn, take a shorter grip on the leash, and bring the dog closer to your side. Repeat the exercise, speaking a sharp-toned *"Heel!"* while using gentle persuasive force to keep the dog by your side. As your Shih Tzu's

This drawing illustrates the proper heeling position. For better control, you should choke up on the leash.

performance improves, take it through a series of straight-line, right-turn, and left-turn exercises. Once it has mastered turning, it is time to begin training on a slack leash.

Perform the heeling procedure with the leash, but do not exert any pressure on the dog's collar. At the dog's first mistake, grasp the leash firmly and lead the dog steadily in the proper direction. Praise it lavishly for its success.

When the dog has learned to walk correctly with a slack leash, it is time to try it without a leash. If your Shih Tzu has performed properly with a loose leash, there is no reason why it should not achieve the same results without it. Do not allow the dog to regress into any bad habits. Whenever it makes a mistake, your Shih Tzu should be given a verbal reprimand. If you continue to have trouble, repeat the *heel* lesson using the leash. It is important to do the exact

Although retrieving is not natural for this breed, it is possible to teach your Shih Tzu this exercise.

same routine with and without the leash. If you do this and remember to praise a job well done, your Shih Tzu should learn to heel properly.

Down

By this point you should have no trouble having your dog assume the sitting position. Grab both of its front legs and pull them forward while saying *"Down."* If your dog attempts to stand up, give it a sharp *"No!"* If pulling on the front legs does not work, try pulling the legs forward while pushing down on the dog's shoulders, using steady pressure. While you are doing this, give the command *"Down!"* Since both of your hands will be occupied, you can carefully step on the leash to prevent the dog from returning to its feet. Keep the dog in the *down* position for about one minute.

As your Shih Tzu progresses, gradually increase the amount of time it must stay down. Once your dog has mastered this exercise, you must begin to move away. As with the *stay* command, move slowly backward while maintaining constant eye contact with your student. If you see the dog begin to stand, repeat the command *"Down!"* using the appropriate tone of voice. Repeat this until your Shih Tzu performs perfectly, making sure to praise it for its good efforts.

Relinquishing an Object

Teaching your dog to give up an object obediently will strengthen your master/subordinate relationship. It is a lesson that every good dog must understand.

Give your Shih Tzu a suitably sized piece of nonsplintering wood to play with and grasp with its teeth. Command the dog to sit, and praise it when it obeys. Then, using both hands, gently pry the dog's jaws apart, while saying *"Let go!"* in a strict and firm tone of voice. If the dog begins to growl, give it a sharp *"No!"* Do not be afraid if your Shih Tzu growls. This is only his way of trying to get you to back down, and thereby establish his dominance over you. Dogs will also growl at anyone or anything that attempts to steal its prey—in this case, the stick. It is important that you make your Shih Tzu know just who is the boss. You must take the object away and establish your mastery. Once the dog accepts you as a dominant force, it will give up the stick without objection.

Keep repeating this lesson until your dog will let go of the stick without you having to use any physical force. Remember to praise it whenever it performs well, and reprimand it for noncompliance. If your Shih Tzu proves to be extremely stubborn, you can confine it to its cage, should all else fail. Upon releasing the dog from the cage, you can try the lesson again.

Retrieving

Retrieving is not an act that will come naturally to any member of the toy-breed group. However, with time, patience, and perseverance, you will be able to teach your Shih Tzu this exercise. In addition to its importance as an obedience skill, retrieving can become a good way for you and your Shih Tzu to play together. The act of retrieving usually demands a lot more energy than the previously mentioned training lessons. So be sure to watch your dog closely, and stop your session as soon as the dog begins to tire.

Start by selecting a suitably sized nonsplintering stick, and have your dog sit next to you, facing forward. Throw the stick forward and call out the command *"Fetch!"* Provided that you did not throw the stick clear out of sight, your Shih Tzu will probably get up and begin to move toward it.

If your Shih Tzu picks up the stick in its mouth and returns to you, command the dog to sit, put your hand (palm up) under its lower jaw and say *"Let go!"* This, however, is not a very likely event. Teaching a Shih Tzu to retrieve is rarely this simple.

If your Shih Tzu shows no desire to return with the stick, repeat the exercise using a thin 30-foot (9-m) rope. Tie the cord to the dog's collar, throw the stick, and again call out *"Fetch!"* Once it has picked up the object, draw the dog toward you, then take the object from the dog while saying *"Let go!"*

You should be able to remove the object from the dog's mouth without any resistance. If the dog drops the stick, or refuses to pick it up in the first place, put it in the dog's mouth and then remove it, giving the relinquishing command. Keep repeating this lesson until the dog understands that the object is to be taken from its mouth.

When you begin the retrieving exercises, you should naturally start by throwing the stick only a short distance. As your confidence in your dog's ability grows, you can gradually increase the length of your throws.

Jumping over Hurdles

Like retrieving, jumping over hurdles is an unusual act for a Shih Tzu. However, it can be learned and later act as a form of play. Start by commanding your dog to sit on one side of a small pile of boards (about 3 inches [7.5 cm] high) while you stand on the opposite side. Command your dog by saying *"Jump!"* If the dog walks around the boards, give it a verbal reprimand, then bring it back and start over. Praise your dog for a successful performance.

Once your Shih Tzu learns to leap over the hurdles on command, you can gradually increase the height of the obstacle. Be careful not to make the boards too high, for an accident could hurt a young dog, and will discourage further jumping.

Once the dog learns to jump the obstacle on command, begin a jump-and-retrieve exercise. Place the stick to be retrieved on the far side of the hurdle. Command the dog to sit by your side. Then command it to retrieve the stick by saying *"Jump! Fetch!"* Make sure that these commands are given in a clear, firm voice. The dog, upon hearing these commands, should leap over the hurdle, pick up the stick, and return over the boards. Tell the dog to sit again, and take the stick from its mouth, saying *"Let go!"* Naturally, such a great effort demands from you the greatest praise.

Training Problems

If, during the course of your training sessions, you should meet a roadblock, remain patient and understanding. Never force your Shih Tzu to learn. Try to keep your sessions enjoyable for both you and your devoted companion. Anger and extreme physical force have never helped a dog learn anything. In fact, they only serve to destroy a learning atmosphere, and will cause your Shih Tzu to lose its confidence and trust in you.

In most cases, you will find that your teaching caused the problem. If, after reevaluating your methods, you feel that this is not the problem, then examine your Shih Tzu and its environment. Perhaps your Shih Tzu is being distracted by an outside factor. If so, then remove the cause before proceeding. If you suspect an illness, make an appointment to see your veterinarian.

If you continue to encounter difficulties, I strongly urge you to contact a reputable obedience school.

Remember to begin training your Shih Tzu while it is still young. However, never force it to learn too much in too short a time. Take your time and make sure the dog understands each lesson thoroughly before proceeding to the next. If you do everything in a correct and timely fashion, there are really few limits to what your Shih Tzu can learn. Unfortunately, it will not be until the dog grows into a mature, well-behaved

adult that you begin to reap the fruits of your training labors. Keep in mind, however, that every ounce of energy you put into training will be given back tenfold. In later years, you and your Shih Tzu will be able to enjoy innumerable hours of wonderful companionship.

Dog Shows and Exhibitions

All purebred dogs such as the Shih Tzu may be entered in any dog show or Obedience competition, provided the breed is recognized by the AKC. These shows are licensed by, and conducted under the rules established by the American Kennel Club. The term "dog show" usually refers to a bench competition, in which a Shih Tzu is judged on its appearance, physical

A Shih Tzu awaiting judging at a dog show.

characteristics, bearing, and temperament. In these competitions, a dog is judged strictly on how it conforms to the Standard for that particular breed, and compared to how every other dog entered conforms to its own Standard.

At Obedience trials, a dog is judged strictly on its ability to perform a special series of exercises. These exercises, chosen beforehand by the AKC, are based upon any work the dog may be required to do. The exercises to be performed are based on a dog's experience in the ring, and may include heel on a leash, heel free, recall, long sit, retrieve on flat, retrieve over a jump, broad jump, scent discrimination, or a signal exercise. While many of these exer-

Whether you show your dog or not, its appearance is a reflection of your care.

cises seem to discriminate against certain breeds of dogs, be assured that the AKC officials try to take all factors into account in order to make the trials fair to all the competitors. An example of this is that when retrieving over a jump, the toy breeds are given a much lower hurdle to negotiate, while the larger breeds may encounter a taller obstacle.

There are other forms of exhibitions by the AKC, such as Field Trials or Herding competitions. However, these competitions are designed specifically for hunting and herding breeds. Because events of this nature are designed to simulate actual hunting and herding situations, it would be impossible for such breeds as the Shih Tzu to compete fairly.

Because bench competitions and Obedience trials have different formats by which they are judged, you should attend them to familiarize yourself with the rules. There is additional information to be gained at these shows as well. Manufacturers of dog foods and other pet products often attend these events in order to better advertise their merchandise. Breeders and dog owners who attend are always ready to exchange tips as well. Quite often, you can also get care and grooming tips from the judges themselves. Even if you choose not to enter your Shih Tzu in a competition, attending a dog show can be a rewarding and educational experience.

If you are considering entering your dog in a show, you will have to supply the judges with your dog's pedigree and AKC registration number, a certificate of health, and an international certificate of immunization.

Showing your Shih Tzu can be a most gratifying experience. Whether your dog wins or not should make little difference to the pleasure you will experience showing a dog in superb condition. After all, your dog's appearance is a direct reflection of your dedication, training, and care. If your Shih Tzu does not win, you should not blame the dog or yourself, for the judging in these competitions is very strict. Just keep your head up, try to correct whatever errors may have been made, and get ready for the next show.

Let's face it: Housebreaking a puppy is definitely not an activity that anyone really enjoys. But if you follow any of the three techniques described here, you will be able to speed up the process while avoiding many of the unwanted surprises.

Paper Training

The objective of paper training is to get your puppy to urinate and defecate on newspapers spread out in an area of your choosing. Naturally, you should choose an area that is easy to clean such as a kitchen or bathroom. Likewise, the area should not be too close to your puppy's eating or sleeping areas, because your Shih Tzu will instinctively try to keep those areas clean and will not excrete near them.

Begin by confining your puppy to the area you have chosen until it voids. If it used the paper, remove the top soiled sheet, and place fresh, clean papers under what were formerly the bottom sheets. By doing this, the scent from the newly exposed papers will be left so that the puppy can relocate the area (by smell) and repeat the act.

If the puppy misses the paper on its first attempt, get the scent of the dog's urine onto a sheet of newspaper and place it on top of the other sheets. Then thoroughly clean the area where the accident occurred. It is important to remove all scent from the inappropriate area that the puppy used so it will not become confused the next time it has to relieve itself.

After eating, drinking, playing, or waking up, your puppy will probably need to empty its bladder and bowels. Young puppies need to relieve themselves every few hours. Oftentimes, the only sign your puppy will give you is that it will begin sniffing the ground for the right place to do its duty. Some puppies may begin sniffing the ground and begin running around frantically, giving you only seconds to react. When this happens, pick up the puppy and place it on the paper in the designated area of your home. You can then gently restrain the puppy's movements until it has relieved itself on the paper.

Then remember the "fifth commandment," and praise your puppy for its efforts.

Crate/Cage Training

Crate or cage training offers a faster and easier alternative to paper training, because it takes advantage of your puppy's instincts to keep its sleeping area clean. If your puppy is wary on its first encounter with the cage, make the cage more appealing by placing some toys inside. Establish a time frame for

A crate or cage can help simplify training your Shih Tzu.

letting the puppy out of the cage. When it is time, take the puppy out of the cage and immediately bring it outdoors to relieve itself. If the puppy has an accident in the cage, confine it there with its excreta for about 30 minutes. By doing this, the puppy will quickly learn to restrain itself until you let it out of its cage. As your trust in the puppy grows and it adapts more to the schedule, you can let it out of its cage for longer periods. Eventually, you will be able to leave the cage door open at all times without fear of accidents, provided that you take your puppy outside as scheduled.

Outdoor Training

Outdoor training begins when you first bring your puppy home. Before taking it indoors, take it for a walk in the area you have chosen for it to eliminate in. Give your puppy plenty of time to do its duty, and praise it for a job well done. Verbal praise and petting will help build your puppy's confidence and will increase your chances of future successful performances.

Most puppies need to relieve themselves as many as six times a day, so you will need to take your puppy outdoors about once every three to four hours. It is also advisable to walk the puppy after each of its meals. When a puppy's stomach is full, it will exert additional pressure on the bladder, so it is best not to wait too long. You should take your puppy for its last walk as late in the evening as possible. This will give you the greatest chance that your Shih Tzu puppy will not suffer any accidents during the night. If you continue to bring your puppy to the same area each time and praise it for each success, it will eventually seek out this area on its own.

Cleaning Up

Although it is true that canine droppings are aesthetically unpleasant, it is your responsibility as a dog owner to clean up after it. Because these droppings can be considered a minor health hazard, many towns and cities have made it illegal not to clean up after your pet.

Wherever you walk your Shih Tzu, carry a plastic bag or "pooper-scooper" with you and dispose of the mess in its proper place. When cleaning your garden or yard, pick up and dispose of the droppings in well-sealed plastic bags in a sealed garbage can instead of burying them underground, because roundworms and tapeworms can be transmitted in the feces. For those accidents that happen in the home, clean with an odor-eliminating disinfectant. Do not use ammonia because the smell may remind your puppy of its urine.

Accidents Will Happen

Regardless of which method of housebreaking you choose, it is inevitable that accidents will occur. If you discover that while you were asleep your Shih Tzu puppy could no longer control itself, remember that it *was an accident*. It will not do you or your puppy any good to get angry or to administer punishment. Puppies have very short memories, so if you do not catch them in the act or make the discovery shortly afterward, a scolding will only confuse your pet. If you catch it in the act, rebuke your puppy with a sharp *"No!"* and then put it in its cage. Never spank your puppy and *never, never, never* put your puppy's nose in the mess. It is not only unsanitary, but it may also upset the puppy to such an extent that you will have a second mess to clean up.

INFORMATION

Organizations

American Society for the Prevention
of Cruelty to Animals (ASPCA)
441 East 92nd Street
New York, New York 10028

American Veterinary Medical Association
930 North Meacham Road
Schaumburg, Illinois 60173

Canine Eye Registration Foundation
South Campus Court, Building C
Purdue University
West Lafayette, Indiana 47907

Humane Society of the United States
2100 L Street N.W.
Washington, DC 20037

Orthopedic Foundation for Animals
2300 Nifong Boulevard
Columbia, Missouri 65201

Therapy Dogs International
P.O. Box 2796
Cheyenne, Wyoming 82203

International Kennel Clubs

The American Kennel Club (AKC)
260 Madison Avenue
New York, New York 10016

United Kennel Club
100 East Kilgore Road
Kalamazoo, Michigan 49001-5598

The Kennel Club
1-4 Clargis Street Picadilly
London W7Y 8AB
England

Canadian Kennel Club
111 Eglington Avenue
Toronto 12, Ontario
Canada

Australian National Kennel Council
Royal Show Grounds
Ascot Vale
Victoria
Australia

Irish Kennel Club
41 Harcourt Street
Dublin 2
Ireland

New Zealand Kennel Club
P.O. Box 523
Wellington 1
New Zealand

The current Corresponding Secretary
for the Shih Tzu Club of America is:
Shirley Merril
3726 Eastman Road
Randallstown, Maryland 21133
Since new officers are elected periodically,
contact the AKC for the latest information.

Books

In addition to the most recent edition of the official publication of the AKC, *The Complete Dog Book* published by Howell Book House, Inc. in New York, there are:

Alderton, David. *The Dog Care Manual.* Hauppauge, NY: Barron's Educational Series, Inc., 1986.

Baer, Ted. *Communicating with Your Dog.* Hauppauge, NY: Barron's Educational Series, Inc., 1999.

Klever, Ulrich. *The Complete Book of Dog Care.* Hauppauge, NY: Barron's Educational Series, Inc., 1989.

Lorenz, Konrad Z. *Man Meets Dog.* New York: Penguin Books, 1967.

Pinney, Christopher. *Guide to Home Pet Grooming.* Hauppauge, NY: Barron's Educational Series, Inc., 1990.

Rice, Dan. *The Dog Handbook.* Hauppauge, NY: Barron's Educational Series, Inc., 1999.

About the Author

Jaime J. Sucher is Director of Research and Development for a manufacturer of pet products. He has written numerous articles on pet nutrition, and is the author of *Shetland Sheepdogs* and *Golden Retrievers*.

Photo Credits

Norvia Behling: 9 (bottom), 12, 16, 17 (bottom), 24, 25, 28, 32, 36, 37, 40, 44, 48, 52, 53, 65; Kent and Donna Dannen: pages 2–3, 9 (top), 17 (top), 29, 60, 64, 68, 72, 73, 76, 80, 81, 85, 88, 89, 93; Tara Darling: page 20; Mella Panzella: pages 4, 8; Toni Tucker: page 56

Cover Photos

Front: Jean Wentworth; inside front: Kent and Donna Dannen; back: Kent and Donna Dannen; inside back: Norvia Behling

Important Note

This book is concerned with selecting, keeping, and raising Shih Tzu. The publisher and the author think it is important to point out that the advice and information for Shih Tzu maintenance applies to healthy, normally developed animals. Anyone who acquires an adult dog or one from an animal shelter must consider that the animal may have behavioral problems and may, for example, bite without any visible provocation. Anxiety-biters are dangerous for the owner as well as the general public.

Caution is further advised in the association of children with dogs, in meetings with other dogs, and in exercising the dog without a leash.

All inquiries should be addressed to:
Barron's Educational Series, Inc.
250 Wireless Boulevard
Hauppauge, NY 11788
http://www.barronseduc.com

Library of Congress Catalog Card No. 99-48388

International Standard Book No. 0-7641-1043-8

Library of Congress Cataloging-in-Publication Data
Sucher, Jaime J.
   Shih Tzu : everything about purchase, care, nutrition, breeding, and health care / Jaime J. Sucher.
      p.   cm. — (A Complete pet owner's manual)
   Rev. ed. of: Shih Tzu. c1991.
   Includes bibliographical references (p.   ).
   ISBN 0-7641-1043-8 (pbk.)
   1. Shih tzu. I. Sucher, Jaime J. Shih Tzu. II. Title.
III. Series.
SF429.S64 S83   2000
636.76—dc21   99-48388
                                          CIP

Printed in China

19 18 17 16 15 14 13 12 11